SAVING *the* LEADER *within*

SAVING *the* LEADER *within*

THE IMPACT OF CHILDHOOD TRAUMA ON LEADERSHIP

Doreen Cato, Ed.D

authorHOUSE®

AuthorHouse™
1663 Liberty Drive
Bloomington, IN 47403
www.authorhouse.com
Phone: 1-800-839-8640

Edited by Regina Chambers

First published by AuthorHouse   12/14/2011

ISBN: 978-1-4685-2558-8 (sc)
ISBN: 978-1-4685-2557-1 (hc)
ISBN: 978-1-4685-2556-4 (ebk)

Library of Congress Control Number: 2011962502

Printed in the United States of America

Any people depicted in stock imagery provided by Thinkstock are models, and such images are being used for illustrative purposes only.
Certain stock imagery © Thinkstock.

This book is printed on acid-free paper.

Because of the dynamic nature of the Internet, any web addresses or links contained in this book may have changed since publication and may no longer be valid. The views expressed in this work are solely those of the author and do not necessarily reflect the views of the publisher, and the publisher hereby disclaims any responsibility for them.

Cover photography created by Ben VanHouten,
Photo Photographer; ben@vanhoutenphoto.com

TABLE OF CONTENTS

"*Saving the Leader Within* demonstrates how one can transform from victim to survivor leader. The story resonates with people who have been victimized physically, mentally and spiritually, and will show that even with years of abuse the human spirit can rise with hope above adversity. *Saving the Leader Within* is an inspiration that shows courage, spiritual and mental stamina will triumph."

Josephine Tamayo Murray, Community Activist

"Having grown up behind a 'curtain of silence,' frequent invisibility and in an environment where 'joy left her soul', Doreen's story is one of transcendence and transformation. Doreen found her voice and her calling and is an inspiration to the many that see her and are touched by her presence, her words and her actions. As an agent of change, Dr. Cato has emerged as one of the great leaders I know, leading from her heart with a passion and expansiveness that calls us all to be and do more."

Shelley Drogin, Ed.D. President, LIOS Graduate College of Saybrook University

"I highly recommend the book to students in college majoring in psychology, as well as adults, who really want to learn to about themselves and life changing experiences and specifically those interested in abuse and how we can stop the stigma in society. Individuals, who are motivated like the author, can move beyond this unbelievable experience if given the opportunity by mentors, role models, teachers, church and the entire village. Hope prevails if we can take care of the individuals who report it and provide the necessary counseling. The author exemplifies the reason to live and succeed if given the opportunity. Please read and pass on to others."

Karen Yoneda, East King County Community Volunteer and Department Assistant at University of Washington

"Finally a new pragmatic insight into leadership development and mentoring, through the reflections of a highly successful leader who has overcome and yet still forever dealing with extraordinary personal trauma."

Kenneth Colling, President & CEO Goodwill

"Dr. Doreen Cato not only triumphs over the traumas of her past, she transcends them. By sharing her story, she shines the light on the key qualities needed for 21st-century leadership—courage, caring, compassion, heart-centered service, and stewardship. Dr. Cato offers a lifeline to others so they, too, can transcend the destructive narrative of their past and create a new legacy of healing, hope, and possibility."

Dr. Gloria Burgess, author Dare to Wear Your Soul on the Outside: Live Your Legacy Now!

"If anyone knows how to thrive despite unfortunate life circumstances, it is Dr. Doreen Cato. She is a leader par excellence and has absolutely refused to let the traumas from her childhood diminish her leadership capacity. And now she tells you how she did it and how you can too. This book is for anyone who needs to know how to see the gift that trauma can be and who has the desire to save the leader within and thereby change his or her corner of the world."

LueRachelle Brim-Atkins, Principal Consultant of Brim-Donahoe & Associates, Inspirational Speaker & Coach

"As a student, teacher and coach of leadership development, I think Dr. Cato's perspective on the importance of one's personal history adds an important addition to the mosaic of leadership development. Her work illustrates how early life experiences, particularly traumatic events that are integrated into the leader's signature presence, can provide a significant foundation upon which the current leadership development approaches can be built. I think it also opens a door into seeing trauma survivors as having the capacity to become leaders, even if it is something they do not yet see in themselves."

Daniel Leahy, past President of Leadership Institute of Seattle, Applied Behavioral Science Masters Program

"Dr. Doreen Cato is one that embodies the spirit of the phoenix and offers the 'deathless inspiration' to thousands of people. Dr. Cato is one of the few people in my life who truly inspires me! In her book, she extends a lifeline to victims to transcend their circumstances into leadership. She eloquently puts into words and names the struggles of guilt, shame, doubt, and fear that enslave victims of childhood trauma. Her tenacity and profound courage to confront the fears that easily entangle many are the impetus that morphs mere survival into thriving!"

Alda K. Yu, Executive Assistant to the President of LIOS Graduate School of Saybrook University

"Get ready for a heart-wrenching and riveting account of Dr. Cato's courageous and silent triumph over trauma—a journey that shows us all how to become leaders from the inside outward."

Dr. Melody Ivory, Inspirational Speaker, Poet, Author & Scientist

"I enjoyed the book and know it will be an asset to anyone studying human behavior."

Deanie Rhoades, Retired Business Owner

"Dr. Doreen Cato has written a compelling, powerful and insightful book about the impact of trauma on historical leaders. Using her own childhood trauma experiences as a lens, she delineates the internal and external factors and interventions that allow one to transcend adverse circumstances and move from victim to victor to leader. Part of the book's power comes from Dr. Cato's compositional style which moves from narrative to meta-cognitive reflections, from memory recall to family interviews that provide contextual explanations, from research to analysis to application. Using her narrative to shed insight on the lives and actions of Dr. Martin Luther King Jr., Eleanor Roosevelt, Sojourner Truth and Wangari Maathai was an excellent choice. If you are interested in knowing about the power of resiliency efficacy, spirituality, social and emotional development and self-actualization from both an historical and personal perspective, then this is a book for you."

Dr. W. Joye Hardiman, Scholar, Educator, Storyteller, Emeritus Faculty & Evergreen State College

"I am humbled and inspired at the power of the work. Without a doubt it will help anyone who commits to improving the quality of life of less advantaged members of our society. The force and candor of Doreen's struggles to maintain her integrity in the face of overwhelming and continuing trauma serves as a touch point for all of us. Doreen's exemplary leadership and her willingness to share herself and her history provides an impetus for all of us to redouble our efforts to help others. Thank you for the opportunity to read this important work."

Harvey Rubinstein, Community volunteer and consultant to nonprofit organizations

DEDICATION

This book is for First Place School and all its children. It is also for my father and two sisters, now deceased, who assisted me with their guidance and truth during the three year research process. Therefore, *Saving the Leader Within* is for Cheryl Elaine Harden Gilmer, Earlene Karen Harden Cranford, and my father Luke Anthony Davis-Harden, *my past;* my brother Reginald Cortez Harden and his family along with my children Christina Cato-Hymes, Zac Hymes, Barron and Misty Cato, *my present;* and my grandchildren Benjamin Daniel Cato, and Mya Charisse Cato, *my future.*

Fifty percent of my proceeds will be donated to First Place School. The mission of First Place: First Place serves families in crisis by providing excellent culturally competent education, housing and support services enabling families to achieve permanent stability.

I really think that the range of emotions and perceptions I have had access to as a black person and as a female person are greater than those of people who are neither . . . so it seems to me that my world did not shrink because I was a black female writer. It just got bigger.

Toni Morrison

EDITOR'S NOTE

Doreen's story compels. Like other greats who have walked a difficult path, Doreen shows readers what leadership born out of chaos looks like. Readers will gain insight into the power of taking responsibility, confronting obstacles and receiving grace. Doreen's story is told through the voice of one powerful soul, who overcomes the forces of fear, trauma and prejudice by channeling a loving vision based in spiritual principles of unity.

Saving the Leader Within is a human story, in the most vital sense, because it also carries universal truth. This book tells the tale of one who takes a painful and difficult journey in order to discover what was always inside, a loving heart and the gifted soul of a person willing to confront the truth and call it by its real name.

Doreen is not a person who is willing to accept the status quo, and has spent her life working to improve the lives of others, through social justice, artistic venues, connecting with others and empowerment. Importantly, *Saving the Leader Within* gives a vivid account of how it is to face traumatic experiences and family relationships with honesty and the desire for growth.

Let this book inspire you to make changes in your life, find forgiveness, seek the truth and commit yourself to a growth path that may include becoming more aware of your impact and how you can make a difference in the lives of children who face overwhelming obstacles. Nothing is really more important.

Freedom is an inside job and *Saving the Leader Within* is an insider's account of Doreen's growth path. The greatest gift of Doreen's research and this story is witnessing the movement of her consciousness from a deeply personal, highly subjective set of memories into the transpersonal and objective realm of true forgiveness.

Regina Chambers, *editor, healer*
Please visit: www.firstplaceschool.org

SAVING THE LEADER WITHIN:
The Impact of Childhood Trauma on Leadership

PREFACE

The brain's function is to choose from the past, to diminish it, to simplify it, but not to preserve it.

Henri Bergson, the Creative Mind, (1911)

There is an abundance of research-based knowledge on the subject of leadership describing qualities a leader must exhibit to demonstrate the ability to lead others. The research done for this book will take readers on an inner journey through the traumatic experiences of my childhood and into adulthood. The events described are placed alongside stories about the traumatic experiences in the lives of four historic leaders. This research focuses on the impact of internal and external influences along with interventions from parents, peers, educators, mentors, and the environment. The critical question that lies behind this work: *How is it possible that some children who experience traumatic episodes transcend to become leaders?*

This book is an examination of traumatic experiences taken from my own life and the lives of my immediate family members, used as a case study. It will take readers on an emotional and mental journey. This research looks at what self efficacy is and its influence in helping a leader transcend traumatic episodes in their past. This case study is significant for two reasons. First, it may help other leaders who carry old scars of shame that surface during private moments of intimacy, child rearing, or when leading others. Second, it will provide insight for educators working with traumatized children by providing solid information about what will help these children move from the stance of victim to leader.

The subjects for this book were my widowed father, two sisters and a brother. Three of whom are now decreased. The research grew out of my ongoing study of our family's history.

ACKNOWLEDGEMENTS

Thanks to all my past, present, and future mentors who stood by me even when I was unaware; special thanks to Ben VanHouten, Photo Photographer, who created the cover; Gina Owens, Karen Yoneda, Emily Dietrich and the Cultural Reconnection Visioning and Planning Team for their encouragement and support.

INTRODUCTION

The real voyage of discovery consists not in
seeking new landscapes, but in having new eyes.

Marcel Proust

The intent of chapter one is to identify elements told through stories that can assist formerly traumatized leaders with their mental and spiritual journeys. On a personal note, this case study will illustrate how doing the necessary research helped me discover my life's meaning and purpose as a leader. Everson (1992) argues, "That the root of all traumas is spiritual abuse, where a young person is cut off from the power that can give him or her life's meaning and purpose" (p. 27), and these words validate my self-discovery. The study discovers how leaders who experienced distressed childhoods managed and transcended those experiences through adaptation, self-efficacy; self-actualization, spiritual and social emotional release. According to DeFrain, Jones, Skogrand, Ernst, and DeFrain (2003):

The journey to health is a long and difficult one, and the early negative experiences appear woven into the individual's very soul, perhaps for as long as the person is alive. As children and young adults, they somehow managed to survive their traumatic time and as adults, they learned how to transcend.

In the case of my siblings and me, two of us struggled to transcend past experiences, move forward and change potentially destructive behavior. Looking back, it is probable that our father's expectations and verbal abuse were partially responsible for our low self esteem. Yet the most damaging culprit became our own inner voice, which had internalized our father's messages, interpreting all the negative experiences. For me, the larger question became, how was my father traumatized as a child? According to Leary (2005), "Trauma is an injury caused by an outside, usually violent, force, event or experience. We can experience this injury physically, emotionally, psychologically, and or spiritually; if trauma is severe enough, it can distort our attitudes and beliefs" (p. 14). On occasion, my father would relate short scenes out of his traumatic upbringing. During our interview he shared, "I was ten years old at the time, when I watched three White policemen drag my mother off the bus. It was the last time I saw her until you kids were born."

When my father was ten years old, my grandmother, a sane woman, was sent to Ypsilanti State Hospital, a mental institution, where she assimilated and lived for 32 years. Today, this would be unheard of as a norm, but *back in the day*, as the old timers would say, during the time of the Great Migration of African Americans and legalization of Jim Crow, this type of scenario was accepted. During my father's childhood, Jim Crow laws were evident in many States in addition to the entire Southern region of the country. After his mother was taken away, my father and his siblings were placed in foster care in Detroit and later sent to Florida to live with his mother's parents. As a college student thirty-five years later, I learned from my grandmother, that the policemen arrested her for dressing as a man and exhibiting odd behavior. My grandmother also shared that her unconventional choices were the only way she could get work in an auto factory and provide for her five children, after her husband's death. Prior to World War

II no woman, let alone a Black woman, was allowed to work in the factories.

Deep inside we knew our father loved us very much and wanted the best for his children. Yet his love also caused us fear. When it comes to raising children it has been expressed many times that children are generally brought up in the same way their parents were raised. Leary (2005, p. 122) adds, "Today we know that if a child has an abusive parent, the likelihood that he or she will grow to be abusive is greater than if that child came from a safe and supportive home." Greene (2002) and Leary (2005) believe physical punishment only produces *obedient* children but does not prevent them from becoming violent or sick adults because of this treatment. According to Alice Miller (1998), this knowledge has now been scientifically proven and in 1998 was finally accepted officially by the American Academy of Pediatrics. Miller also states:

> Maltreatment and childhood abuse without intervention can produce terrible outcomes. Studies document that ". . . a child beaten often and deprived of loving physical contact would quickly pick up the language of violence. For him or her, this language becomes the only effective means of communication available . . . when I tried to expose the social consequences of child maltreatment I first encountered strong resistance. Repeatedly I was told, I too was a battered child, but that didn't make me a criminal. When I asked these people for details about their childhood, I was always told of a person who made the difference, a sibling, a teacher, a neighbor, just somebody who liked or even loved them . . . through his presence this person gave the child a notion of trust and love.

In response to this statement by Miller, during a face-to-face interview with my youngest sibling I asked a question that opened a closed door for both of us. I asked, "Why did you choose a different path in life and not attend college?" I was unprepared for my younger sister's response. Until that day my other siblings and I believed our youngest sister had experienced an easier life than the rest of us. For most of her formative years, she lived away from the verbal and physical abuse we received, or so we thought. Below is an excerpt from our face-to-face interview in July of 2004:

She was silent for a moment and began to say something about why she took this different path, then broke down and cried. It was hard and moving for me to see her crying, *even now as I write about this experience my eyes are misting over with tears because I know how painful her life has been.* She began again and said:

I wanted to go on but I was discouraged by dad constantly telling me that I was not going to amount to anything. This was on top of being separated from all of you for 7 years. Even though I lived down the street from all of you, it still hurt to see you all together on the porch laughing. I thought no one wanted me. When I returned to live at home permanently, I was eleven years old going on twelve and you were leaving that summer for college. Little did we know you were leaving for good and I know how hard your life was under his physical and emotional abuse, where you had each other I was alone. I did not think highly of myself then and began to believe that I wasn't going to be anything, so why try. This led me to John, my first husband, who was also abusive and a heroin addict. After two years of hell, my daughter and I escaped his abuse.

As you know, I later met my current husband and that is when my life started to change. I think dad must have seen his role in what was happening in my life; at least that is what I want to believe when he decided to send me out here to live with you (p.22).

This forgotten memory and revelation lead me to rethink my own journey and especially how messages from my father and others in the community had affected our lives. My sister for example perceived these messages as weapons whose intentions were responsible for where her life path had ended. This innocent inquiry fueled an intense interest in me to examine other compelling social and personal implications (Moustakas, 1990, p. 27).

According to Brooks and Goldstein (2005) child maltreatment can cause depression and intense sadness or irritability that can disrupt concentration, sleep, eating, and energy levels. In many cases, maltreatment can lead a child or youth to feel hopelessness. On the other hand, DeFrain (2003) states, "It has been estimated that between one-third and more than two-thirds of children who have been abused do not grow up to become parents who abuse their own children" (p.4). This finding is supported by other studies on relationship by Egeland, Jacobvitz, and Strufe (1988); Hunter and Kilstrom (1979); Steele and Pollack (1968), and Straus (1979).

However, intergenerational abuse did occur in our family history; my father was raised by an abusive grandmother whose mother was a slave. This abuse was condoned by a grandfather who was a former slave. Both grandparents knew no other way to discipline but through the sting of a bull whip and humiliation; something they experienced at the hands of their White masters or overseers. For my siblings and

Doreen Cato, Ed.D

me it was the sting of an electric cord and humiliating messages. Leary (2003) states, "The slave experience was one of continual, violent attacks on the slave's body, mind, and spirit. It is a known fact that slave men, women and children were traumatized throughout their lives and the violent attacks during slavery persisted long after emancipation."

My father shared how he endured the severe beatings and other cruel punishments inflicted by his own parents and grandparents. He also shared how he and his siblings were unable to adapt to the southern Jim Crow rules in place at the time. He managed to leave Florida at the age of sixteen to rejoin relatives in Detroit. Leary (2005) points out how in most slave families the dominant male is generally the father or as in this case the White master or overseer. Leary states, "It was the master who more often than not became the imprint for male parental behavior and this imprint was passed down through the generations; at its foundation, this imprint was dominated by the necessity to control others through violence and aggression."

In line with this, my father's stories about his childhood life, wartime experiences, and escapades before and after marrying our mother were equivalent to listening to old mystery episodes of "The Shadow" on the radio. In various stages, through his stories, we became somewhat desensitized to or inoculated against the racism and discrimination we faced each day. Peters (1985) as cited by Greene, Taylor, Evans, and Smith (2002) provides a definition given to him regarding the inoculation and desensitization of children:

Although parents may be challenged by what can be the debilitating effects of bigotry and prejudice, they can successfully socialize their children by transmitting values and teaching adaptive strategies that make it possible for their children to succeed.

The face-to-face dialogues were emotional and took me as the researcher in a different direction. These dialogues introduced a new level of awareness into my family relationships by encouraging authentic conversations between us. These discussions were a refreshing experience because they broke through our old pattern of guarded and superficial conversation.

Two of my father's favorite messages are positive memories from my childhood that will always remain with me, first: *You are somebody so keep your head up high because we come from a proud race of people.* And second: *There is no such thing as a closed door; the only closed door is the one in your mind. Remember, all doors have keys; you just have to find the right one.* One story comes to mind about a time when both of these messages played a crucial role in my adult life. It was during my race for public office as the only candidate of color in a hotly contested race for city council. Campaigning in predominantly white neighborhoods where many opposed my platform was difficult, but my father's message to *keep my head up* stayed in my mind. Also, my logo for the city council race depicted a key on a chain and whenever I gave a campaign speech I found a way to mention my father's message about how there is *no such thing as a closed door.* These internalized messages gave my spirit strength and resilience in the face of obstacles.

Parental messaging is a powerful tool whether given directly or indirectly. Two African American child psychologists, Martin and Martin (1978) state, "Child rearing in Black family tradition rested upon religious beliefs, strict discipline, respect for parental authority, and reliance on authority." In their ethnographic study they also acknowledge that the elders believe children should be reprimanded or punished by any member of their extended family if they are disrespectful to authority; children are also expected to stand up for what is right, and protect their own blood. I remember when my father schooled me about protecting my siblings and my body. He said, "If anyone hurts you or your sister and brother, it's your duty to defend yourself and them. I better find them in worse condition than you." Leary (2005) notes, "Invariably our parents, families, and friends play a vital role in helping us form our image of ourselves." This statement is well in keeping with how my father raised us. We each developed unique personalities in the silo of our home. According to Richardson (1995) author of Family Ties That Bind, "Each family member develops a unique personality, but not in a vacuum. Your personality develops in response to the other personalities in your family." Richardson also notes, "The way individuals balance themselves or create imbalance in their family determines the general health and happiness of all the family members." This helps explain how my sisters, brother and I all triggered each other with our general moodiness and depressions. This phenomenon also showed up when any one of us contracted measles, chicken pox, or colds—we usually all got sick at the same time. My father also helped this process along with the herbal concoctions he would use to treat us. It was too costly for him to miss work on four separate occasions, and so when one of us became ill with an infectious disease; he made us all drink hot ginger ale mixed with some kind of root he took from the backyard. The next day we would all be sick.

Regarding trauma, I have experienced how an old phenomenon becomes unconsciously real when a leader dealing with a stressful situation gets triggered. This case study focuses on elements of phenomenon, which defines things that we perceive as real or not. Phenomenology is a science that goes straight to the heart of the matter. It consciously seeks out the basic nature of an event without reference to the question of what is real or not. (Merriam 1998; Patton

1990) When a person or one's body remembers a traumatic event, he or she will relive that painful incident experiencing the same emotional and physical responses of the past. It is important to remember that memories of that past traumatic moment are also full of distortions, due to the passage of time and the age of the person when experiencing the original event. The person tends to remember the trauma on the mental, emotional and physical level, and not always in sequential order. This adds to the phenomena that trauma brings. Our bodies hold emotional memories of traumatized events as snapshots of unsuccessful attempts to defend ourselves in the face of threat and injury. (Levine, 1996) The final element of this investigation was to review existing research on notable leaders and the characteristics associated with leadership. My research concentrated on Sojourner Truth, Dr. Martin Luther King Jr., Eleanor Roosevelt and Wangari Maathai; noteworthy leaders who each experienced a traumatic childhood. Through my research, I gained insight into their painful life experiences and also what allowed them to transcend these experiences in order to lead. The knowledge gained from this part of the investigation was inspiring. I approached this research with the question, *Was it the mentors, education, and or spiritual growth that made it possible for them to transcend their traumas?* As I studied, I learned that each of these elements assisted these well-known leaders in transcending their painful histories and becoming the historical role models we admire today.

My journey begins in chapter one through an inquiry process of self-discovery—the immersion phase. The discovery process helped me to reach back and unveil what my unconscious memory retained. In following chapters, the intensity of my immersion in the past lessens as these formerly unconscious memories slowly take shape. In addition to the unfolding development of my memories, the recovery experience provides great insight and allows an objective look at my family's history. Through this step, I released old memories as well as the emotional and physical pain my body held trapped inside. *Even now as I write this down and begin to give voice to the secrets, my head is pounding and my abdominal muscles are tightening, but it is time to tell this long overdue story.*

CHAPTER ONE

THE CASE

You got people out there with this scar on their brains, and they will carry that scar to their graves. The mark of fear is not easily removed.

Ernest J. Gaines, The Autobiography of Miss Jane Pittman

This case covers the lives and experiences of one African-American family comprised of a widowed father and four children, ages nine, eight, six, and three at the time of their mother's death. Immersing oneself in exploring the unconscious, helps to surface past experiences (Moustakas 1990). Using this process I relived experiences from the age of three to adulthood, using statements taken from interviews with my father and siblings. Quotes from case studies, personal journals, and autobiographies of known leaders are incorporated. This led to the discovery of how these selected individuals transcended their traumatic childhood experiences to become renowned leaders.

Making the Case

My family's story in this immersion phase is shared in its purest form without interruptions or clarifications. It was necessary to come to intimate terms with why only two of my family members were able to transcend their childhood traumas, in order to live, grow and be productive, regardless of the past. Our story starts when at the age of three I was separated from my family and stayed in the sanitarium ward at the County General hospital to be treated for tuberculosis. I later learned from my father, the length of my stay was eighteen months. This information gave me insight and began to fill gaps in my memory. When I was put in the sanitarium, my parents had only two children; my younger sister and me. At the time I was unaware that mother was already expecting my brother. On the day I was left at the hospital my father unknowingly relayed a powerful nonverbal message to an impressionable three year old. My extended stay at the County Hospital at such a formative age explains many of the institutional behaviors I adopted such as unconsciously waiting for permission and finding comfort in being alone. During my time in the hospital I learned to keep to myself, rarely speak unless spoken to, ask permission before going to the bathroom and push people away who tried to hug me. Upon my return home my father expressed strong disapproval of these learned behaviors.

This is how it all began for me. It is a gray and cold day, but I don't care because I am with my mother, father, and younger sister in the back seat of the car. My mother gives me an orange, but I am too excited about the ride in my father's car to eat it. I hear my parents speaking in hushed tones about something that is causing my mother to cry and I sense it is about me. I stop for only a moment to wonder if it has anything to do with my cold. I quickly say, "Look mommy I'm eating my orange." I cough as quietly as possible so not to disturb my parents in the front seat of the car. *In writing this passage I suddenly noticed how my thinking process and tone revert to that of a young girl.* The car comes to a sudden stop, and little did I know my world was about to change forever. My dad turns to my mother and asks if she wants to take me inside, I saw her head shaking no and she continues to cry softly. Something tells me I am in trouble and so I tell them both that I am ok and that I will eat my orange like a good girl. *At the time I was unaware that I was infected with tuberculosis.*

Watching the nonverbal drama unfold between my parents was how I began to be observant of more than verbal cues. I would experience many later traumas in life behind a curtain of silence. The memory of this day is so vivid it is like yesterday. As I look back in my mind's eye, it appears as though everything was happening in slow motion—starting when I left the safety of the car, and looked back to see my mother and sister waving goodbye to me. Seeing the look on their faces frightened me most of all. My mother's sad face spoke the loudest—I knew something was going to happen.

As I reflect back on this moment I realize now that my mother's strong nonverbal message spoke to me long before the following incident with my father played out. I find myself gaining clarity about my father not being the only player in this traumatic incident. It becomes clear that my mother played a significant role in this traumatic day as well.

My father had a strong grip on my hand as he walked silently by my side towards this very large brick building. The immense size of the building really stood out on that gray and dreary day, but I had a deep trust that my father would protect me as long as I was with him. Entering the building with its wide hallways, I remember looking at how empty and uncluttered they were with a few chairs for my father and me to sit on as we waited. A White man came out of the office and motioned to my father to join him, they too spoke in hushed tones. *Again I notice my writing has shifted to the voice of a young girl.* In my memories up to this point, this was only the second time I remember seeing a White man. A White woman joined this man and my father motioned to me to go to him. I did and once I was near him the White strangers grabbed my hands tightly, then my father turned around without a word and began walking away. *Even now at sixty-two, I feel the tears welling up in my eyes as I remember this awful moment in my life.* I fought with all my might and screamed for my father not to leave me. He would not turn around. I thought if I could get him to turn around everything would be alright and I could go home. Yet no matter how loudly I screamed or how hard I fought, the many hands prevented me from breaking away. The only thing that mattered to me was that my father would not turn around when I cried out *Daddy*! The person I trusted left me with these strange looking people. I was abandoned and alone. Once my father was gone they strapped me down to a table and forced a tube into my nose asking me to swallow. The pain was excruciating and then I felt a sharp jab followed by darkness. When I awoke my mother was sitting by the bed. I thought she was there to take me home. Instead she fed me soggy cornflakes that soothed my sore throat. My heart was broken and it was too painful to cry anymore. Later, at age sixteen, I learned that the nurse had called my parents that day and asked them to return. The nurse told my parents she wanted me to wake up and recognize someone familiar and that they were worried about putting me into the large ward right away. *This tells me the nurses were concerned about my emotional and mental well-being.* I remained in the hospital from the age of three until I was five years old, a total of 18 months, and internalized many messages of hopelessness, despair and fear. These were permeating emotions that I was unable to differentiate, articulate or understand at the time. It all felt like loneliness. It was here that joy left my soul. *Naming the memories of loneliness, despair, and hopelessness are from my adult recollections more than my childhood memory.* Freud cited by Gardner (1991) "Once claimed which has long since become common knowledge that the experiences of the first five years of childhood exert a decisive influence on our life" (p. 110).

Eleanor Roosevelt was a surprising find when I started researching historical leaders. I was led to Eleanor Roosevelt's story from a statement made by Howard Gardner. In *Leading Minds: An Anatomy of Leadership,* Gardner (1996) describes Eleanor Roosevelt as "Often positioned politically left of her husband, Franklin D. Roosevelt, she became the lightning rod for criticism."(p. 7) Gardner's statement intrigued and inspired me to see if there were other elements that affected her life.

CHAPTER TWO

ELEANOR ROOSEVELT

"I think that somehow, we learn
who we really are and then live
with that decision."

Eleanor Roosevelt

Many people would ask how could Eleanor Roosevelt have had a traumatized childhood, how could that be? She seemed to have everything a girl in her social circle could hope for: privilege, wealth, a distinguished family lineage, and world renowned relatives, such as her uncle, President Theodore Roosevelt. Yet it is important to keep in mind that trauma sees no social category, ethnicity, class, gender, age, disability or economic condition.

Eleanor Roosevelt was born in 1884 and died in 1962. She was born into a family of generational wealth and prestige, but also one that was ravaged by alcoholism, substance abuse, and self-destruction. According to Blanche W. Cook (1992, p.38), Eleanor's childhood was a time filled with anguish and tragedy.

She also states,

Like most children of alcoholics, Eleanor felt that she could never do enough to protect her father, to care for him, to ward off danger, to change or try to control the situation. But she never knew when his eruptions of rage, self-pity, or despair might occur. (p.39)

Eleanor romanticized her relationship with her father and began to feel estranged from her mother, who was known as a great beauty. Eleanor absorbed the negative messages her mother sent such as, "you have no looks so see to it that you have manners."(p.62) External and internal messaging is also what brought self-doubt, low self-esteem, and depression to my siblings and I. Believing the negative messages passed along to us by our father and neighbors instilled self-hatred in all of us. In some situations this may have been similar to what Eleanor experienced when she found it impossible to please her mother.

There was a particular traumatizing incident that stayed with Eleanor throughout her life. According to Cook (1992, p.48), at the age of two and a half, Eleanor, her nurse and parents boarded the ship Britannic on their way to Europe for an extended tour of the continent. The following is what happened on the first day out:

There was a fog that blinded the Celtic, an incoming streamer, causing them to ram their ship. Suddenly they were surrounded by screams of agony and hideous sights of carnage. One child lost an arm, another child was beheaded. Many passengers were killed, hundreds injured. Her father Elliott Roosevelt helped his wife, sister-in-law, and the baby nurse into a lifeboat, and then called little Eleanor, clinging to a crewman, to drop her into his waiting arms. But Eleanor would not let go. She screamed and

7

cried. The din all about her was terrifying. Eleanor's abiding memory was her profound fear of being dropped from the deck into her father's waiting arms. The crewman finally freed her fingers, and Eleanor always remembered that fall, the feeling of plummeting from the deck high above into the pitching lifeboat below, surrounded by cries of terror and shouts for help.

A memory of that terrifying night returned later when she was subjected to one of her father's obnoxious outbursts when she was unable to go down a steep incline on her donkey. She could see his disapproval when he leaned over and said, "I never knew you were a coward" (Cook, 1992, p.58). Since she was so close to her father, this statement must have been crushing. He rode off leaving her there at age five to think about her failure and how she had disappointed him. Cook (1992) discovered a description of this incident in one of Eleanor's memoirs. Cook (1992) also noted, "It seemed never to occur to Eleanor, even years later that her father's expectations had been unreasonable, and his impatience cruel." (p.58) Neither Eleanor nor her father were able to recall that the distance of the steep incline may have unconsciously caused her body to remember that terrifying night when she was dropped a great distance into her father's waiting arms.

There were protective factors that appeared to be missing or in deficit during Eleanor's childhood such as caring relationships, positive messages, and opportunities to feel productive, useful, and of value. She experienced much emotional and physical abandonment by both parents. Although she forgave her father, this caused her a great deal of depression and feelings of despair. During one such situation of abandonment, Eleanor's mother was awaiting the birth of her second child (Elliott Jr.) and wanted to protect Eleanor from the tension and her father's suicidal behavior. For these reasons Eleanor's mother placed her in a nearby convent (boarding) school. Cook (1992, p. 63) cites what Eleanor wrote about that time period:

> "The house in Neuilly was small, so it was decided to put me in a convent to learn French, and to have me out of the way when the baby arrived. In those days children were expected to believe that babies dropped from Heaven."

Eleanor longed for attention, warmth, and love during this time in exile. She even drew attention to herself by pretending to have swallowed a penny because another child really had done so. Her mother, predictably, reacted with anger and the nuns did not treat Eleanor as they had treated the other child who had swallowed a penny. Instead they sent for her very pregnant mother to come and retrieve her because she had told a lie; lying was considered a sin and justified expulsion from the convent. *This episode in her life takes me back to my own exile as a hospitalized three year old who felt similar emotions.* Acting out her frustrations during this incident was only the beginning for Eleanor. Expressing her anger and disappointment over feeling emotionally and physically abandoned by those she loved may have actually helped to save her from other physical ailments caused by stress. Cook (1992, p. 19) describes Eleanor during this stage, "Eleanor became sullen and grew stubborn and spiteful." She would deliberately disobey her mother, lie about her behavior, steal candy meant for her parent's dinner guests; and when her mother tried to take her to family or friends' parties she would have a sobbing tantrum and refuse to attend. Through these antics Eleanor found a way to rid herself of some of the unhealthy stress in her life. All of this occurred before the age of eight, and as Cook (1992, p. 22) writes, "Both her parents and one of her brothers had died by the time she was nine years old."

Let's remember that Eleanor Roosevelt eventually became the wife of a U.S. President, mother to five children, an author, feminist, social justice and civil rights activist, civic volunteer, philanthropist, political genius, and mentor to many women and men. Eleanor achieved these accomplishments with the help of many who mentored and encouraged her along the way. After the death of both parents, Eleanor's mentors renewed a sense of love and trust; one such mentor was Marie Souvestre, who had a school in England. At the age of fifteen Eleanor was sent to this school by her grandmother, Mary Hall, where she stayed until she reached the age of eighteen. Eleanor blossomed under Souvestre's tutelage and became more confident, independent, sophisticated and outspoken. In a protective environment, Eleanor embraced self-efficacy, spirituality and nurtured her own emotional development. It was also under Souvestre's influence that she learned the ability to adapt. When it came to her spirituality, Cook (1992, p. 5) writes, "Eleanor Roosevelt frequently spoke and wrote about what spirituality meant to her: she participated in an undefined ethic that embraced the world community. It was not about fear and damnation or about any specific knowledge or duty. Rather as Eleanor stated: "'In the infinite extent of the universe it is a direction of the heart.'" *It is remarkable to me as I write these words how spirituality has taken on a whole new meaning in my life.*

A White Ally

C. S. Brown, (2002) author of *Refusing Racism: White Allies and the Struggle for Civil Rights,* defines White ally citing Beverly Tatum

(1994), "[a]n antiracist activist, a White man or woman who is clearly identifiable as an ally to people of color in the struggle against racism" (p. 5). Brown identified Eleanor Roosevelt as such a person who "took the leadership in fighting racial discrimination at the national level." Eleanor Roosevelt had her internal fight with color and racism, and won. This was remarkable considering the fact that after the death of both parents Eleanor's grandmother raised her in a racist environment. Brown (2002) points to Eleanor Roosevelt's first term as First Lady and how she initially referred to her Black staff as darkies and pickaninnies. Yet, after her travels and through her friendships she became conscious of discrimination and its devastation on the Black community. She also saw the discrimination continue in the New Deal programs. President Roosevelt was heavily influenced by Eleanor and laid the foundation for later presidents and generations to continue the fight for equality in public policies. Brown (2002) also states that it takes courage to resist White supremacy. Eleanor's willingness to provide an intervention in the plight of the Tuskegee Airmen made a mark and was a turning point in the war. At the time, during the beginning of World War II, a group of accomplished young Black men were unable to fly because they had been deemed incompetent and unreliable by White generals and officers. Eleanor shot this theory down by going to the airstrip where these men were trained and asked them to demonstrate their ability with her aboard. For this the African American community has been forever grateful.

Informal Dialogues

Information gathered about Eleanor Roosevelt's background left me hungry for more knowledge of my own history and why my father did not come back and get me on that horrible gray day when he dropped me off at the hospital. To retrieve this information in a caring way from my father required some doing, since he had also hidden his true feelings about that day. Using informal dialogue as my approach with family members during the research process encouraged authenticity and self-disclosure from everyone. During this series of dialogues symbolic growth occurred for both parties. For example, the altering experience of learning what happened to my father on the day he left me with the doctor and nurses. The following dialogue was taken from my March 2005 taped discussion with my father. Here I identify myself as the researcher.

Researcher   Dad do you remember that first day when you left me at the hospital when I was three?

Father: Yes, it was the worst day of my life.

Researcher: I remember screaming for you to come back and I could not get you to turn around. Remember?

Father: Yes, how can I ever forget it? Baby, I knew if I turned around I would have gone back and got you (he stuttered with a catch in his voice) which would have been the wrong thing to do because they told us your TB was in the critical stages. Going back to get you would have cost you your life.

This last piece of information my father revealed made me feel as though icy cold water had been poured over me. It dawned on me that as an adult I had carried an incomplete memory as the barometer for how much my father loved me. From the perspective of a small child I thought he did not love me because he left me at the hospital and through our adult dialogue I learned he did. I know that at this early age I was unable to comprehend what the devastating effects of tuberculosis could do to my lungs. *While writing this last statement, a chill passed through my body, because I just realized that by taking me to the hospital for treatment my father saved my life and that leaving me there was probably the hardest thing he had to do.* Five years later after our mother died, my father had to make another, another difficult and similar decision about my youngest sister when he decided to leave her in the care of our neighbors.

The albatross of rage began to lift from my shoulders and I found myself really seeing my father for the first time without the filters of abandonment and rage. This was one of the reasons I chose to immerse myself in the past. These filters were part of my unconscious thoughts that may have prevented my father and me from having authentic conversations up to that point. The immersion process, by slowly probing my unconscious, helped me to surface memories. The process of going deep inside to remember pieces of my story required quiet and seclusion from outside distractions. My family's story is interwoven to include the stories of each family member along with the messages we each absorbed from mentors, peers, educators, and the surrounding cultural environment. Through sharing memories I discovered how past perceptions and messages from others had influenced my thoughts and affected my life.

There was sadness for me in conducting this research because of the deaths of two of my siblings that occurred during this investigation, leaving only my brother and I alive to remember and bear witness to our family history. The trials and tribulations we all endured as a family finally took its toll. Even though their passing was particularly devastating for me and is even now too painful to remember, I find myself asking what elements prevented me from taking a similar road in life as my departed siblings. It took a statement cited by Ungar (2004) to address this for me, "Exactly where a child will find his or her path to resilience is difficult to say." Nevertheless, my decision to survive and pursue the question '*How is it possible that some children who experience traumatic episodes transcend to become leaders?*' prompted me to open old wounds. These old wounds were reopened during the discovery process. During discovery I wondered how those historical leaders managed to consciously or unconsciously find ways to transcend the crosses they carried.

It was at three years of age that I first lost joy. After watching my father leave and the subsequent fight on the examination table, I awakened in a hospital room to find my mother by my bedside. I later learned, at age sixteen, that hospital staff called my parents because of the trauma I had undergone. I had hoped my mother had come to take me home, but she fed me soggy cornflakes instead. This was the beginning of a long separation from my family. The hospital ward with the many other children became my home and family. It is so hard to remember much of my time there, yet I do have strong memories of three events that impact how I relate to others.

The first event took place on a gray afternoon, when the nurse brought our food trays in. I always referred to these nurses as the ladies in white. Before I entered the hospital, my mother had taught my sister and me how to recognize colors. At the time, I was three years old, going on four. I could only move so far in my small space, because of the white restraint jacket that was tied to the top of the bed. The ladies in white also brought the toy tray around for us to select toys to play with before dinner. That day I chose a White doll with a blanket that I secretly kept hidden under my covers so I could cuddle with it later. Yet this was not to be, because the food I ate caused me to have diarrhea. It came on so quickly that I was unable to call out for the nurse to help me on the pan. I remember feeling so scared. I knew I was not supposed to make a mess in my bed, because the ladies in white would punish me. I tried to hide what had happened with the doll blanket, but this only made the mess worse. I guess I did not realize that the nurse could smell what I had done, but nevertheless, I was shocked when she came to me with an angry looking face and snatched the bed covers from me. The other children in the ward became silent and I think that scared me more than my accident. I knew something else was going to happen and it did. She took away the doll that I was going to play with after dinner. I learned a new rule that day, no matter what, don't hide the mess and call the nurse as soon as possible. I also learned to expect very little kindness and compassion from adults.

This new place had more rules than I had at home. As soon as they arrived in our ward and before we were served our food we had to raise our hands to let the nurses know we had to go to the bathroom. I learned to recognize the daily routine which was the beginning of my conditioning. I knew when mealtime was over, because they always gave me a shot with a long needle afterwards. The toy tray came before our lunch and after dinner. *I just realized that I wrote the word tray which is an old word used for the toy cart.* And again, we had to let the nurses know if we had to use the bedpans when they came to take the toy cart away. Afterwards they would warn us before turning out the lights by saying lights out and telling us that we were to be quiet or else.

A poem entitled Fear taken from *The Book of Qualities* (Gendler, 1988), speaks to what this nightly warning meant to me:

Fear has a large shadow, but he himself is quite small. He has a vivid imagination. He composes horror music in the middle of the night. He is not very social, and he keeps to himself at political meetings. His past is a mystery. He warned us not to talk to each other about him, adding that there is nowhere any of us could go where he wouldn't hear us. We were quiet. When we began to talk to each other, he changed. His manners started to seem pompous and his snarling voice sounded rehearsed.

Fear was with me every day. Even to this day, the fear I felt between the ages of three and five passes through me at night. As I remember those evenings and the night sounds that made the ward look so different and so frightening a fearful chill washes over me. Back then, I always pulled the covers over my head at night, and still to this day at 62 years old, this is something I do when I awaken during the night to house sounds and distorted shadows on my wall.

Loss and Grief

A second event at the hospital unconsciously taught me about loss and grief. The memory of this incident only returned during a classroom exercise while participating in a Masters program at Leadership Institute of Seattle (LIOS). Several of us were participating in what is called a fish bowl. This exercise placed me and several peers in the center of a circle while the rest of the class observed our interactions. Something we did in that group-setting triggered the memory of an event so traumatic that it was previously locked away from my conscious memory. I remember mentally pushing against a heavy black door to keep it closed. The door had a sliver of blinding white light peeking out from behind. But the door burst open and I blacked out. The memory came roaring back unbidden. Then, according to witnesses, my speech regressed to the level of a four to five year old child; my left hand was suddenly groping behind me as though I was trying to reach for something; and I began crying in the voice of a little girl. When this occurred, a LIOS faculty member in the room leapt over chairs to my assistance and cradled me in her arms. The smell of cigarette smoke in her sweater revived me; my mother had also been a smoker. This is the memory I shared with my classmates and teachers:

In the hospital ward my playmate after lights out was the boy assigned to the bed next to me. Our beds had wheels that allowed us to move them when the nurses were not looking or were out of the room. They were designed to prevent us from falling out of bed as were the jacket restraints tied to the head boards. We would move our beds together at night to play between the side bars, quietly giggling and whispering to each other. We did not want to wake up the older children in the ward, who would tell on us. One night after lights out, I pushed my bed close to my friend and reached out to play with him. I could not get his attention. I sensed without knowing that something was wrong. He did not respond. His stillness made me cry. I guess my crying must have been pretty loud because a nurse came in and found us together. The nurses immediately separated us and began pulling my bed out of the ward, and when I turned around to see if they were pulling my friend out as well, they were putting the cover over his face. I tried to reach behind me *this is what the students at LIOS saw* to take off the restraints so I could get out of my bed and be with him, but I could not remove them. I cried even louder. The nurses took me to the room where they kept the bath tub and our toy cart. I was alone and scared, which made me cry even harder. I cried so long that my throat hurt. The nurses came back in after I stopped crying and pulled my bed back into its place in the ward. I remember feeling pain in my stomach when I returned and the worry that I was going to have an accident in my bed again, but I did not and curled up under my covers. My friend was gone forever. I learned another lesson that day, that it was not ok to show grief, and that doing so would only bring you more. This loss taught me how much I had cherished my friend's love. I mourned the loss for the rest of my stay in the hospital.

This crushing experience taught me not to make friends, and that it was safer to play with toys and talk to grown-ups, who went away but always returned after awhile. As a grown woman, I found my voice of that time, well described in the *Book of Qualities (Gendler, 1988)*: "Never have I heard such sounds of weeping as when Grief found out her son had drowned. She screamed and howled. She stamped her feet and smashed her pots and bowls. She ate with all of her fingers. She tore at her hair, and it grew wild and matted. She wandered from place to place with no sense of where she was or how she came there." The memory of that night was hidden deep inside the recesses of my mind and was one of the worst traumas of my hospital stay.

The Sacrifice

When I was five years old another memorable event happened when I was scheduled for my twice weekly treatment. It was the same treatment I received on my first day at the hospital. This involved hospital staff removing mucus from my chest area by shoving a rubber tube down my nose and asking me to swallow. I hated this procedure with my whole little being. It was very painful. I knew my treatment was coming because of the piece of colored paper they placed at the foot of my bed. I waited for the nurses to leave the ward and for lights out to push my bed to the child lying next to me and trade my piece of colored paper for his. I had found someone to sacrifice. The next morning I was awakened as my bed was pulled out of the ward to deliver me for the very treatment I was trying to escape. I looked at the nurse and said "Not me, him." I remember trying to figure out how they discovered that I was the child who was scheduled to receive the treatment. I grew older and continued to ask myself this question. Of course, over time I came to realize that it was because the hospital staff could read and at that time, I could not.

These memorable events and the verbal and nonverbal messages I received shaped my future behaviors. As a small child I could only interpret them with my limited understanding of the world around me. The eighteen months I spent in the children's ward of the Wayne County General Hospital were traumatic and left me with a terrible emotional legacy. There were two things I remember being fearful of at night: having my bed pushed against the wall for fear that the large bugs, cockroaches, would eat me; and the different sounds that night brings. I also knew the jacket restraint would prevent me from escaping. The big kids added to my fear by waiting until the nurses left to tell the little kids that the jacket restraints were to keep us from falling into the crocodiles' mouths.

Homebound

William Pickens was a well-known educator and advocate for civil rights who once said "living together is an art." This quote fills my mind as I look back and remember the day I left the hospital to return home. I remember being afraid of the family I would rejoin, yet who I barely knew. When I first saw my sister and two-year-old baby brother they were holding onto each other tightly. They were afraid of me. I later learned, during my interview with my sister, that when I first returned home she thought I was going to hurt them and she was protecting our brother from me. What irony since I was deathly afraid of them. I did not know that life at home would be so different from the hospital or that I would have only four short years of time left with my mother. When I arrived home on that first day, I remember sitting on the living room couch. My father was excitedly showing me two belts, explaining how he purchased one for my sister and one for me. My mother intervened and asked him to slow down. In all of this chaos, I raised my hand for permission to go to the bathroom, but no one noticed. I did not know where the bathrooms were in the house to go on my own and I had not been allowed to go anywhere in the hospital without permission from the nurses. I accidentally urinated on the couch, which made my father very angry and caused an argument between my parents. This is the vivid memory I have of my first day home from the hospital. I immediately withdrew from this chaotic scene into silence. *Finding solace in solitude had become my way of overcoming a traumatic experience.*

Unbeknownst to me at that time, one month before my release from the hospital my mother received a diagnosis of Lupus. Yet, when I came home I remember feeling so excited when she told us the news that a new baby was coming. My mother must have noticed how I envied the relationship that my younger sister and brother had, because she promised I could name the next baby. I was six years old at the time and remember naming the baby as being very important. Due to my mother's illness my youngest sister was born three months prematurely. I ended up naming her Earlene, after my cousin and me. I was nine when my mother died; four years later.

It hit us all hard when my mother died. I was so angry at her for leaving me that I refused to cry at the funeral. This behavior baffled the adults who I overheard communicating their displeasure about my performance at the funeral to my father claiming I did not care about her death. I failed to cry and throw myself on my mother's coffin. I was angry because she left me with the person I feared the most, my father.

Hard Lessons to Learn

My father was a stutterer and abusive and hollered at our mother all the time. At the age of five, I thought he hated me. I had evidence to support this. Every day for example, it was our mother's responsibility to teach my four year old sister and I lessons. Then, when my father returned home from work, he would make us stand in front of him and recite our colors, the alphabet, and count to ten, or sometimes to twenty. My sister was ahead of me because our mother taught her while I was in the hospital. I was playing catch up. I remember one evening in particular when he came home and wanted me to perform my lessons aloud like my sister and expected to hear me recite the alphabet. My mother had worked all day with me, but when my father returned home that night I just could not remember the letters. He ordered me to stand in front of him and make an effort, and as I struggled in fear, he took off his belt. My mother pleaded with him to give me more time, but he said he knew how to make me remember. Every time I missed a letter he would hit me, until he reached a point when he was so angry he grabbed my hand and began beating me without restraint. I could hear my mother screaming at him to stop. She finally got me away from him and the next thing I knew she had me outside and was telling me to breathe. This same scenario was repeated often. Another instance that stands out in memory is when he wanted me to learn how to ride a bike. These were hard lessons and instead of learning how to love and embrace my family, I learned to live in fear and dread.

On another front, my father did not want my mother taking me to the Herman Keifer Hospital, known for its work in tuberculosis, for my T.B. shots. These were the shots I required in order to fully heal after I left the hospital. She would ask me not to tell my father and sneak me away to the hospital for my shot once a month. My mother was my protector who would always try to shield me from my father's rages and abuse. I gained this understanding after overhearing my father tell my mother that he believed those treatments would keep me sick. She eventually stopped taking me to that big looming brown brick building for my shots, but only after I received the full course of treatment.

I was not the only target for my father's rage, he would physically abuse my mother also, which sometimes caused mother to run away with one or all three of us. The last time mother ran away, she took my brother. When our father found them both missing, he piled the rest of us in the car and sped off to find her. He found out which bus she took and went after her. He caught up to the bus and they fought. She and our brother returned to the car crying and I remember wondering if she could protect me anymore. This was my second year back home.

My mother died two years later. I remember her last day with us. It was the same day as her death, when the hospital gave my father permission to bring us to see her. This was an unusual privilege as it was against hospital policy to have children visit the terminal ward. The following is taken from my personal journal:

When I went to kiss my mother, she was so very hot and dry. She was much darker than what I remembered when she was last home. My mother held me tight and whispered in my ear, "to remember to make sure my brother and sisters ate their vegetables." She also wanted me to promise to include some kind of starch and meat in the diet. I became frightened and asked her when was she coming home? She kissed my forehead one last time and asked to see my sister Cheryl. After either speaking to or holding each of us, she signaled to the nurses and our father who picked up the baby and led us to the car. This was the last time I saw my mother alive because the next morning I overheard my father on the phone saying our mother had died. I was nine years old.

CHAPTER THREE

SOJOURNER TRUTH

Then I will speak upon the ashes.

Sojourner Truth, when told of a threat to burn down the hall where she was about to speak.

Deflowering of Innocence

It was at the age of ten that my father's friend who we called Uncle sexually molested me. He was a pedophile. My sister, who was the second oldest, was molested first, and kept this a secret from all of us. I only knew that she had been acting differently for two months leading up to my molestation experience by Uncle. I had noticed that she refused to wash or to set foot near Uncle's home even when our father threatened to punish her. I will never forget the night of my own terrible experience at his hands. Our father was working a late shift and it was my responsibility to make sure my siblings stayed in the house and were fed dinner. *It is funny what one tends to remember.* My eight-year-old sister was standing on the stool staring out the kitchen window while she was washing dishes. The night was humid because it was the month of July and the sun was starting to set. I noticed we had eaten all the sugar and knew how our father would want his cold drink

24

of lemonade waiting in the refrigerator when he came home. I turned to my sister and said I was going over to Uncle's home down the street, to get some more sugar. She turned to me and said in a monotone, "I wouldn't go if I were you." I asked her why, but she would not respond. I thought she was jealous, because for the past week Uncle had been treating me nicely and not talking to her anymore. I wish that I had listened, because I bounded across and down the street to his house, not knowing Uncle's wife was not at home. Once I was inside, he took my empty cup and grabbed me. As I recall this moment in time, I can see the shadow of the sun setting in his kitchen and smell his breath on my face has he forced his lips on my for a kiss. I fought with all my might to get away from him but he was too strong. He managed to kiss my mouth and push his tongue inside. Because I was so small his mouth covered most of my face. I remember not being able to breathe through my nose or mouth. I thought I would suffocate. I remember crying silently; not making any noise. The ringing of his telephone stopped him from going any further. I was literally saved by the bell. *I am noticing how my shoulder and back muscles have tightened up as though I was pushing away from something. My body remembers.* He held on to me even when he answered the phone but I broke away from his grip. I do not know how I broke away, but I did and ran home. My sister was still at the window and without looking at me she said, I told you not to go over there. My thoughts centered on what we were going to do and also the question of who would believe us.

An Uncaring Community

After the outrage of that first sexual molestation at ten, Uncle made sure the next eight years were a living hell. He had a key to our home and knew our father's working schedule. *My heart is hammering as I tell this next part.* The worst nightmare was waking up in the middle of the night with him standing over our beds smiling down on us with his white teeth. We would wake each other up and scream for our brother, who was three years younger, to help us get this man out of our house. He would finally leave, laughing because he must have known that no one would believe us. We believed the adults in our community had given us up to this man to save their own children because no one came to our aid. It was easier for them to deny the ugly reality, call us whores to our faces and forbid their children to play with us. There was one incident during this horrible period that made our father a hero in our eyes. It happened when my father came to our defense against a neighbor's accusation. My sister and I had been attending a neighborhood gathering with other children. This adult announced to everyone at the party that my sisters and I were bad girls and let men do terrible things with us. *We did not know what she was talking about or that she was drunk at the time.* She then turned to us and asked in an angry voice to leave her backyard because our kind was unacceptable in her home. We left crying and went running back to our house. When our father returned home from work that evening, we told him what had happened. He did not say one word to us, but marched across the street and loudly told both of the neighborhood women who were sitting on the porch that if they told one more lie about his daughters he was going to sue them. This was the first time I ever heard our father come to our defense against the cruel things said about us. We were so proud of our father that day.

Much later, on my wedding day, I learned from the very neighbors whose children were forbidden to be around us that they knew about Uncle. They wanted me to forgive them for their previous judgments and lack of caring action. My research led me to the Search Institute, where I learned that one of forty positive assets that contribute to the healthy development of a young child is a caring community. The caring community asset occurs when a young person experiences the caring of neighbors. This asset was entirely missing for us during this tumultuous time in our lives. I often wondered what kept us sane, until one day I came home from school and found my younger sister trying to attempt suicide. She was eleven years old. My brother and I stopped her by breaking the lock on the bathroom door in our effort to prevent her from ever doing it again. *We never told our father what had really happened that day, even though we both were severely punished for damaging the door.* We bandaged her arms to hide the cuts and made her wear long sleeves for weeks during the summer. When we asked her why she wanted to take her life we came to learn that our father's friend had confessed to her best friend's mother that she was sleeping with our father. As a result, her mother asked my sister to leave their home, because she considered her to be a bad influence on her daughter. I can still hear her crying while telling us this story. *I am writing this with tears streaming down my face.* I used to ask God at night in my prayers why were people so cruel, and what had we done to deserve so much cruelty? I can hear my nightly prayer in my head. It was the one my mother taught us. This prayer gave us all great comfort, "Now I lay me down to sleep. I pray the Lord my soul to keep. If I should die before I wake, I pray the Lord my soul to take." We worried and wondered constantly about our youngest sister, who had the most exposure to Uncle. We referred to him as the monster. We constantly begged our father to let her come home to stay arguing that I was old enough to take care of her. He did not allow her to return home until I was eighteen and it was my last year living at home. When we would ask our younger sister if she was alright, her response was always, *yes.*

It was not until she was thirty-two years old that we learned the truth about her rape at the age of ten. As children, we often speculated that the neighbors knew the truth about this man and gave us up to protect their own children. We were the scapegoat for this community, who refused to let their children play with us because they considered us to be a bad influence. These are the words the neighbors would say directly to our faces, in front of their children. Ironically, the neighborhood children knew this accusation was not true and would sneak to play with us anyway. *Could the decent behavior these children exhibited be considered an intervention?* I believe it was one of the only saving graces of that time; knowing that someone believed us. *Is this an example of a caring community even though it was comprised of children? How we were able to overcome this challenge in our lives is a mystery. Or did we?*

One day we convinced two of these young friends to hide in our coat closet, knowing it was around the time that Uncle would come by for an envelope my father had left for him. After he came inside, Uncle saw that our brother was not home and so began his sexual assaults and our friends heard our struggles to fend him off. What we failed to realize was our young friends were just as helpless and unable to change the situation. Yet, there was power and strength in knowing we had done something to resist our fate. There is so much more to tell, because this story does not end there. Many years later, on my wedding day, one neighbor who had warned her daughter not to play with us, quietly took me aside to apologize for her actions and ask my forgiveness. All I could think was *how dare she try to ruin my special moment.* I was too full of rage to accommodate her wishes that day.

Discovering Personal Power

We were trapped. Our father's friend was considered a leader in the community, but he was a predator. He had already begun his campaign to discredit us by telling others in the community that we were liars and liked older men. He had convinced his own family and even our own father that we were liars. This was later vocalized by another one of my father's friends at his gas station, when I was fourteen buying gas for my car. *Yes, I was driving the back streets to the grocery store then, because my father was working two jobs and was unable to shop, so he taught me how to drive.* That day, I went inside the station to pay for the gas when my father's friend closed the door then proceeded to try and rape me. I remember struggling in silence. Finally out of frustration he confessed that he had been told that we liked older men. When I broke away from him, I asked him from a safe distance who told him that. This is when I learned what our father's friend had done. Fighting back became a powerful solution and offered a way to regain control over what happened to me.

I shared a revealing face-to-face dialogue with my sister, the second oldest child. This particular sister had received more interventions than our youngest sister. She had been very successful in both her business and community endeavors. She had received several awards and recognition for her leadership from the Mayor of Detroit and the Girl Scout Council. Both of my sisters had taken on visible leadership roles in the community, one as a nationally recognized Girl Scout Leader, and the other as the creator of an accomplished drill team consisting of children of color. To the external world they were accomplished and confident leaders. Yet, in spite of these wonderful accomplishments, it was how they felt on the inside that took a mental and emotional toll.

It took my informal face-to-face interviews with my sisters for them to recall certain disturbing incidents in their lives. The second oldest girl's discussion about her second suicide attempt brought out much of what had been going on inside her. As we continued to reminiscence about our childhood, I asked her these questions:

Researcher: "With all that happened to us why do you think you and I are where we are today?"

Sister: "We're fighters. It's not about giving up or laying down, or finding excuses, we're fighters."

Researcher: "What do you remember about trying to kill yourself at age eleven, would you have considered that giving up?"

Sister: "What about that day you ran away would you consider that giving up or fighting back?"

Researcher: Yes, but it made me stronger, when I returned full of resolve to finish school and then move out.

Sister: Well, I would call what I did abusing myself more than trying to commit suicide. I was hurting inside and all I wanted to do was make it stop. Abuse is all I knew. When you and our brother stopped me from hurting myself any further and wrapped my cuts I knew I was loved and made a quiet promise to never do that again. I took charge of my life after that even at eleven. It was then that I was determined to leave Our Lady of Lourdes and start over.

Two years later my sister did leave Our Lady of Lourdes and without permission from our father enrolled at Cass Technical School. At that time, Cass was one of the top high schools in the nation. My sister's statement and the resolve she showed, is validated by DeFrain, et al (1998), who writes:

No matter how dysfunctional a family may be, they are also likely to have some strength that can become the foundation for healthy new directions; a crisis in life can be a catalyst for positive growth. In essence, there is always some reason for hope, no matter how desolate one's life may appear (DeFrain, 1999; DeFrain & Stinnett, 2002; Olson & DeFrain, 2003).

For my siblings and I, strength emerged as the ability to fight back. For example, my sisters and I discovered our own personal power around choice and resolve. This resolve appeared early in our lives without conscious awareness. It emerged when we decided to stop a relative's sexual abuse. We had another uncle, an actual relative who was also a pedophile and who was married to our favorite aunt. During the weekend, we went to their home while our father worked his second job. This second horror show in our lives took place when I was between the ages of ten and twelve. My aunt was my mother's best friend and we loved her dearly. She loved us as well but we avoided telling her what was actually happening at our house or in her home. We were ashamed, and beginning to believe we were at fault for what we were experiencing.

When we did try to tell aunty about her husband our situation only worsened. It was a disaster, mentally scarring her daughter, our cousin, for life. It was in the evening when my siblings, our three cousins and I were sitting around the kitchen table talking quietly amongst ourselves about our uncle (our cousins' father). My aunt and uncle were entertaining company in the next room. There was a swinging kitchen door that separated us from the living room where they socialized. That night all of the girls were angry, because we knew our uncle would sneak in later to take one of us, including his own daughter, out of the bed to sexually molest. Since my aunt was poor, all four girls slept in one bed. We would protect my youngest sister, who was three at the time, by placing her close to the wall.

That night, we persuaded our female cousin, who was eight at the time, to tell her mother what her father was doing. We did not know that we picked the wrong time for her to attempt this terrible task. She went in the living room and loudly got her mother's attention. Then, once the room was quiet, she said *"Mommy can you tell daddy to keep his hands out of my panties."* It would not have been possible for the room to get any quieter than it did. Then we heard a loud slap and our cousin fell back through the kitchen door with a red welt on her face. The part that frightened me the most was when she managed to pick herself up off the floor and without saying a word to any of us sit back down at the table and begin eating as if she had never left the table. Following in suit, we all returned to the table and finished our dinner in silence. We had learned what we could say and what we could not say to adults.

During the following years, I remember my father trying his best to make sure we had as normal a life as possible in spite of his erratic work schedule. For vacations we traveled by car to New York, Pennsylvania, Ohio, and Illinois. We four kids were the happiest being together as a family on the road away from the craziness. Throughout this time our father had no knowledge that we were being molested. The incident at my aunt's had been a powerful lesson in maintaining the silence. We knew one thing for sure, we were on our own. I silenced my voice, feeling a sense of resignation and agree with Gendler's (1988) description when she writes, "Resignation would rather curse the darkness than light a candle. At first she intimidated me, now she infuriates me (p. 7)"

Resigning ourselves and accepting that our fate was sealed left us in the position of protecting ourselves. We chose different directions in terms of how we went about staying safe; two of my cousins adopted a tough guy persona and succumbed to drug use; my female cousin, sisters and I went emotionally numb. This numbness can be described as the act of burying our emotions so deeply inside that others had difficulty determining if we were feeling anger, fear or frustration. My female cousin's past experience and my own unconsciously caused our marriages to fail. Sojourner Truth, one of my heroes, experienced rape, brutality and unspeakable grief. Her life story makes me wonder whether she, like my cousin, siblings and I, chose to endure in silence to get through similarly traumatic episodes.

According to Nell Painter (1996), author of *Sojourner Truth: A Life, A Symbol,* Sojourner Truth was a leader in the women's rights movement in the 1800's. During that era, one White minister declared publicly his belief that only men should have rights, as Jesus had been a man and not a woman. Truth's response to this claim reflects the leader within. As stated in "Ain't I a Woman?" her retort, "I have borne thirteen children and seen 'em mos' all sold off to slavery, and when I cried out with mother's grief, none but Jesus heard me! And Ain't I a Woman (Patterson, et al, 2000)?" In spite of the traumas she had incurred and in a time when most African-Americans were still enslaved she fought for two causes: equality and freedom for all women. Sojourner Truth was a traumatized child who became a leader among those who enslaved her.

Historical Background

In the 1790's Sojourner Truth's given name was Isabella the slave. She later changed her last name twice. After leaving her slave owners land without permission and claiming her freedom, Sojourner moved in with Isaac and Marie Van Wagenens, a White Methodist couple in Ulster County, New York. The Van Wagenens found a way to make her freedom legal (Painter, 1996, p.25). Although the couple opposed slavery, to prevent Isabella from being returned to her slave owner, they purchased her themselves. They then freed her. After the Van Wagenens purchased her from slave owner Durmont for $25 ($20 for her and $5 for her daughter Sophie), Isabella adopted their last name Van Wagenens or Van Wagner outside of the county. Isabella's first language was Dutch and she first learned English through her other slave masters prior to her time with Durmont. Painter (1996, p. 15) states, "Isabella was an abused child and her strategies for survival resembled those of other abused children. As is often the case, she found ways to explain away and excuse the abuse. For example, Sojourner once said, "I can verify the truth of this statement and remember being in such a state of depression that I thought the assaults on my body were meant to be and that I was doing something to make them happen." (p. 15)

Before her time as a renowned abolitionist, feminist, singer, and preacher Truth experienced severe losses and oppression. Her traumatic childhood was filled with the oppressive societal ills and violence that regularly accompanied slavery. As a child, Truth was repeatedly raped and sexually molested by Durmont and his wife until she reached adulthood. According to Painter (1996, p.17), the Durmonts subjected Isabella to multifaceted abuses that destroyed her self-esteem and distorted her reality. Their perpetuation of physical and sexual abuse eventually blurred into justification for her existence. At some point, they forced her to marry. Through this union Sojourner gave birth to five children, only to lose two. One child was auctioned off to a different slave owner and the second child died. Losing these children devastated Sojourner. Although the State of New York allowed the slaves to work off their indentured servitude, by the time Truth was eligible to acquire her freedom she was unable to leave with her husband or all three of her remaining children. Instead she left, taking only her infant daughter Sophie. The two remaining children and her husband were still required to work off their debt separately.

Truth's second youngest child, Peter, was one of the two children she lost. He was a five year old boy who was sold twice before the age of six. A year after leaving the plantation, Truth learned of Peter's last placement with a viciously abusive slave owner who was a relative of her former master. Upon learning this, Truth went to court to get Peter back. Even as a freed person of color this move in itself was unheard of. Yet the court ruled in her favor and returned the child to Sojourner. During the exchange between Sojourner and the slave owner, when the young child saw his mother a distressing incident occurred. According to Painter (1996) an eye witness account describes how the child screamed and cried clinging onto his abuser. Peter clearly wanted to stay with his abuser rather than go back to his mother. I empathize as a mother and can only imagine what Sojourner must have felt in that moment. I also have empathy for the child, and directly understand the terror of being returned to people with whom you have little or no consistent bond. *I remember it felt safer to remain at the hospital—than my own home. Could that be why after returning home I was ill most of the time?* According to Painter (1996, p.34):

Isabella (Truth) had no way of knowing Peter's response after so tragic a separation was characteristic of children who feel themselves abandoned by the adult to whom they are most attached, no matter what the objective circumstances of the loss.

When I read Painter's analysis of what happened to Sojourner in that exchange I experienced an explosively insightful revelation; it vindicated my confusion about why my anger towards my father was so intense. One can only imagine the hurt and embarrassment Sojourner must have felt in that moment of rejection by her son. Yet she still managed to take Peter home with her and through her strong convictions and with support from the religious community mother and son survived the ordeal. Sojourner's accomplishments demonstrate how one can transcend the traumatic episodes in life to eventually self actualize.

Painter (1996) believed Sojourner's strength came from a *secret power* that Black women possessed and passed down through generations to counter the negativity they experience in the world. In most religious communities this is known as sanctification or a blessing. The hope and belief in a higher spirit is what Truth admittedly thought provided her with the ability to act and adapt. As Painter (1996, p. 41) writes: "More than anything else she did or said in her life, this ability to act with the support of a powerful supernatural force and to mine its extraordinary resources made Sojourner Truth a representative African-American woman."

Sojourner became a model for all women and with her belief in civil rights for women obtained notoriety among the antislavery social workers of that era.

In 1827 Isabella along with several others founded a church called the Kingston Methodist Church. As a preacher she was known for her ability to dazzle listeners with her wit and charisma. She was considered a 'here and now' presenter who was seeking immediate change. Painter (1996) points out that Truth was known as an unsentimental straight-talker. Painter also cites how Truth's accomplishments demonstrated her aptitude to be original, creative, independent, spiritual, and her ability to adapt. Painter (1996) writes how Sojourner's dedication to and belief in God's constant support released her from the crippling conviction that she was nothing. Painter (1996, p.22) describes three dimensions that gave Sojourner freedom and I believe these to be characteristics derived from the protective factors identified below:

When she thought the time was right, she left the plantation to claim her freedom. *(Self-efficacy)*

She freed herself from fear through a discovery of Jesus' love and empowered by her new religious faith. *(Spirituality)*

She broke out of the passivity of slavery by using the law toward her own ends. *(Self-actualization)*

And most importantly, her ability to continually adapt (*Adaptation*)

These dimensions identified by Painter helped Sojourner transform herself from an evangelist into an anti-slavery feminist. Painter (1996, p. 25) points out that Truth's religious foundation is best described as influenced by rural people in New York and New England; a blend of beliefs and habits from animist West Africa and pagan Europe, The Calvinist Dutch Reformed Church and the Armenian Methodists.

Truth's new found strength was evident when she spoke out in the speech *Ain't I a Woman* against those who stood in the way of women's rights. At the time, women like Sojourner were commonly scorned by men who believed they were more characteristically male than female, which may have prompted her speech. Truth believed that gaining rights for women would empower them in many ways. She believed it would make a difference for women to receive proper wages, receive an inheritance, hold office, attend schools for higher learning and professions; and gain custody of their children. Truth probably thought and hoped that her fight would pave the way for her people to receive freedom. Leary, author of *Post Traumatic Slave Syndrome* (2005) believes that ingrained messages can inhibit our ability to survive and thrive if we do not reexamine or replace these messages as necessary. In the legal proceedings involving Truth and her son; Sojourner could have chosen to act in a self-deprecating manner about her essential worth and the worth of her son. She could have made apologies to the judge and verbally devalued her son, in the common stance of a slave, while simultaneously protecting her child from placement in the hands of another slave master. This common slave practice involved outwardly camouflaging the worthy qualities of their children when faced with the threat of their purchase and removal by White slave masters. However, Sojourner chose not to send these messages, and was awarded custody of her son. In today's American society we no longer allow slavery, but traditional messaging practices from that era often carry on as they are passed down, with their origin often unrecognized, through African-American families with a heritage of slavery. Today, many recognize that outwardly devaluing the character or traits of a child while he or she is within hearing distance may be considered emotionally and mentally abusive and wounds the child's self esteem.

My siblings and I for example were sometimes unable to transcend the negative messages we heard so often in our youth, because we internalized them as the truth and did not reexamine the messages.

Sojourner Truth died on a cold gray day, November 26, 1883. She is long remembered as a public figure, social activist, and feminist of her day. Her life experiences and choices shaped her legacy which speaks of her fortitude and compassion for others.

CHAPTER FOUR

OPPRESSION, RACISM AND CLASSISM

I have a dream that my four little children will one day live in
a nation where they will not be judged by the color of their skin, but by
the content of their character.

Dr. Martin Luther King Jr.

Oppression is pervasively woven throughout many U.S. social institutions. This hideous disease is often embedded within an individual's unconscious, in addition to being consciously perpetrated. It is described as more than discrimination, bias, and bigotry, but as an insidious and pervasive infection that can overpower and shape a person's life. Oppression is sometimes beyond an individual's control; a situation in which dominant or privileged groups consciously or unconsciously benefit. According to hooks (as cited in Greene 2002, p.249):

The oppressor group also has control of resources and dominates the choice of cultural and linguistic forms used in a social structure. As a result of this domination, the group lacking power and resources are at the margin or outside the main body of society. People at the margin may develop a sense of futility or feel hopeless, helpless, or estranged.

Conscious knowledge of oppression entered my life when I was fourteen. I had an experience that comforts me to this day. In June of 1963, something wonderful took place and for a brief moment in time I felt special. I had recently read in the *Chronicle* about a great man who was coming to Detroit to lead a march down Woodward Avenue. Planning to participate, I worked hard for two months to save my weekly allowance so I could look good on that day. When June 23, 1963 arrived I was so excited. I had just laid my new clothes out on the bed, when my father called me downstairs to let me know that he had been called into work and I had to cancel my plans to go downtown. I was so upset. Then I was determined that this was not to be a day when I would give in to my father's wishes. I was willing to suffer the consequences and be punished. I waited until he left for work and ran across the street knocking on neighbors' doors to see who would watch my brother and sisters. Finally I found someone to watch them. I missed my scheduled ride, but had enough allowance money to catch the bus to Woodward Avenue. I will never forget that hot day in June. I remember being overwhelmed by the number of people that were waiting to march with Dr. Martin Luther King Jr.; I never could have imagined there would be that many people. I learned later we were over 100,000 strong that day. I was unable to find the family I had planned to join, but a lady grabbed my hand and said, "Honey there's no strangers today." She led me to a long line of people and this is when I saw Blacks, Whites, Mexicans, Chinese, and people from other ethnic groups I did not recognize linked arm in arm. This was remarkable because it was the first time in my life that these groups were not fighting or calling each other names. I remember turning around and trying to see everything. I did not want to miss anything, the blueness of the sky or the stickiness of the tar on the street. I wanted to remember it all, because this was the best day I had experienced in such a long time; a day when I felt good about myself. The horn blew and the surge of the crowd carried me as we linked arms singing "We Shall Overcome." I did not know it then, but I was making history, because this was the largest march Dr. King had led up until that time. It was two months before he led the historical march on Washington D.C.; of course I did not know that then and probably would not have cared. After the crowd reached the front of Cobo Hall, Dr. King began his speech and sent the message that inspired me to eventually dedicate my life to social justice:

> "The price that this nation must pay for the continued oppression and exploitation of the Negro or any other minority group is the price of its own destruction."

It was after this statement that I looked around and was surprised to see so many White people marching with us that day; it was uplifting to hear Dr. King acknowledge their presence. In an autobiography by Carson, et al, (2001), Carson mentions how Dr. King Jr. said in his Detroit speech that day, "They tell us that the Negro and his allies in the White community now recognize the urgency of the moment."

After Dr. King finished speaking, I quickly ran to catch the bus for home before my father returned and found out I had disobeyed him. That night I watched the news to catch a glimpse of the great man. I felt really proud that day. That short moment in time made all the hurts and pains go away. I can only imagine what a slave must have felt when they realized the chains were off for the first time. I found my voice of courage that day. Dr. Martin Luther King Jr. (1967) said it best when he said, "Oppressed people cannot remain oppressed forever. The yearning for freedom eventually manifests itself, and that is what has happened to the American Negro."

I realize now that Dr. Martin Luther King Jr.'s message was not just for the White people, but for everyone who discriminated and perpetuated injustices upon others. Dr. King's message was uplifting to many people who worked in the factories with little or no education. Even though our father had not finished high school, it was important to him that we were well-educated. He never let us forget how his mother, our grandmother was once a teacher in Philadelphia and our own mother had more than a high school education. Dr. Martin Luther King Jr. was the savior and hero of my community.

CHAPTER FIVE

DR. MARTIN LUTHER KING JR.

M-mm-mmm, should we demonstrate, tolerate,
educate, negotiate or just kick-ass . . . ?

Mona Lake Jones, Ph.D., (1993) *The Color of Culture*

Dr. Martin Luther King Jr. experienced what many believe to be an exceptional childhood. He was born in his grandparent's home in Atlanta, Georgia on January 15, 1929, given the name Michael, which he later changed to Martin, and died on April 6, 1968.

His father, Martin Luther King, Sr., was a sharecropper's son who suffered all the horrors of post Civil war tyranny and institutional racism and encountered brutalities first hand. His father always expressed an interest in civil rights. In one instance, as a young person when Martin Sr. brought to his father's attention that the White boss-man was cheating him, the White man quickly chastised his father calling his son a nigger. Martin Luther King Sr. made up his mind to leave the farm when he was older. He also managed to get his high school education by the age of eighteen, and finished his education with a degree from Morehouse College. Martin Luther King Sr. was a great man to emulate, especially when it came to the rights of others. Martin Luther King Sr. was president of the NACCP, and later in Atlanta led the fight to equalize teachers' salaries. He was also instrumental in eliminating Jim Crow restrictions on elevators in the courthouse. Yet, his father had another side, and like my own father had been exposed to intergenerational abuse.

What many do not know about are the many experiences in Martin Jr.'s childhood that exposed him to racial hatred, humiliation and physical abuse from his father. External messaging from his father and the constant incongruence of his environment contradicted his mother's conviction that he was able to do whatever he wanted to do.

According to Howard Gardner (1995, p. 204) author of *Leading Minds: An Anatomy of Leadership*, Dr. Martin Luther King Jr.'s "father had no qualms about beating him, it was the only standard disciplinary behavior his father knew. To make his son a better man, he would beat him regularly, and his mother and grandmother would console him afterwards. In addition to the physical abuse, it appears that the younger Martin had twice tried to take his own life." The young Martin attempted this immediately after Jennie Williams, Martin Luther King Jr.'s grandmother, died of a heart attack on May 18, 1941. Her death happened during a Woman's Day program at her husband's Church. The death was traumatic for her grandson, especially since it happened while he was watching a parade against his parent's instructions. In his distress and grief, he leapt from a second-story window of the family home. Although he was not seriously injured, he wept on and off for days and had difficulty sleeping. In his book, Frady (2002, p. 14) also cites the two suicide attempts when he states:

He early showed an inordinate compulsion to take on himself great cargoes of guilt, which impelled him, twice before he was thirteen, to bizarre gestures of suicide both times leaping out of a window over an unbearable grief about his grandmother, whose most cherished grandchild he always knew he was. The second time, having slipped away one Sunday to watch a downtown parade, he instantly supposed that this little delinquency accounted for his grandmother's death by heart attack that afternoon, and he flung himself with sobbing abandon out of the second-floor window of the house.

However, as an adult Dr. Martin Luther King Jr. tried to bypass that era in his life by stating how unremarkable his life had been prior to the civil rights movement (Gardner, 1995). It is not uncommon for children who have experienced a trauma to block it out, and it is possible this explains his later stance. According to Carroll (2005), it is common to consciously repress unpleasant experiences. Many psychologists believe that an unconscious repression of traumatic experiences, such as sexual abuse or rape, is a defense mechanism which backfires. The unpleasant experience is forgotten but not forgiven. It lurks beneath consciousness and allegedly causes countless psychological and physical problems from bulimia to insomnia to suicide.

Carroll's statement speaks to my sister's suicide attempts. She was never willing to discuss with us the specifics of her sexual molestation experiences. This secret she harbored was knowledge that I believe drove her to self-destruction.

Dr. King Jr.'s unwillingness to forgive his father's actions also validates Carroll's statement and may help explain why Dr. King Jr. made his second suicide attempt.

Clearly, protective factors such as caring relationships, positive messages from his parents and the community, along with opportunities to speak helped make Dr. King Jr. feel productive, useful, and of value. His sense of self value was evident in his academic performance. He skipped several grades to enter Morehouse College at the age of fifteen. Greene (2002 citing Bernard (1993) states that "A summary of study outcomes suggests that resilient children have a strong capacity to form relationships, to solve problems, to develop a sense of identity, and to plan and hope" (p. 5) Wolin and Wolin (1993) also identified seven resiliency factors derived from survivors who shared their childhood adversities as insight, independence, relationships, initiative, creativity, humor, and morality. Interestingly, Dr. King also exhibited these characteristics as a leader of socio-economic causes, an advocate for the poor, a pastor in his own church, an anti-war activist, as well as a committed husband and father. Protective factors as described by Greene (2002) are "Conditions that buffer, interrupt, or prevent problems from occurring" (Rutter, 1985, p. 4). The initial protective factors: adaptation, self-efficacy, spirituality, and self-actualization are believed by most resilience theorists to help individuals transcend traumatizing childhood episodes. The protective factors that perhaps stood out the most for Dr. King Jr. were spirituality and emotional development.

Dr. King's spirituality and emotional development were nurtured through the messages of praise given to him by his parents, teachers, and a supportive community as well the praise he received later in his adulthood (Gardner, 1995). He had caring relationships with many people, in addition to his parents who also passed on positive messages, through which he was made to feel productive and valued. This is right in line with what Rutter (1985) identifies as protective factors that build resiliency. Sojourner Truth was also a trauma survivor who credited positive messaging with leading her to the Pentecostal faith. Sojourner believed these positive messages were responsible for bringing value to her life (Painter, 1996).

As Taylor Branch (1988) describes in his book, *Parting the Waters; America in the King Years, 1954-63, a*s an adult, Dr. King Jr. came to a personal crossroads when he was asked to act as a leader beyond his church, when Nixon, one of the organizers of the Montgomery boycott, approached him and asked for his participation. At first, Dr. King was reluctant to participate, but then tapped his courage from within. He reconsidered and stepped out to the front of the church to speak without notes and inspire the church meeting attendees. According to Frady (2002), "It was the most dramatic instance yet of King's sharing that mystic capability of leaders of genius, at certain critical moments, to suddenly transmute into someone, something, awesomely larger that their ordinary selves" (p. 35). This is a great example of Dr. King Jr.'s adaptive skills in a situation where he was initially hesitant to step forward. His ability to adapt in a special moment created a sweeping movement for generations to come. We are still reaping from his courage today. *I can't help but wonder if his courage will continue to reach into the lives of my grandchildren's children's grandchildren . . . I do wonder.* I do know that his ability to adapt and self-actualize eventually gave a nation an opportunity to dream.

Racism

When it was time for my youngest sister to enter school she was sent to public school for kindergarten since the Catholic school started at the first grade. This decision was a double-edged sword. We did receive a strong educational foundation from the Catholic school we attended, but at what price? Up to this point my brother was spared from sexual molestation, but not from the racist behavior of the White nuns and lay teachers, as well as racial harassment from other students. This harassment was in addition to the daily bullying and humiliation he took from individuals in our own community. Our father's friend must have taken lessons in degradation which he bestowed heavily on my brother. It was catch-up time for him. My brother was the darkest of all of us and the most handsome. He had a beautiful dark brown complexion that framed the whiteness of his teeth when he smiled and the sparkle in his eyes demanded your attention. As time went by, I rarely saw that beautiful smile or the sparkle in his eyes. Someone had turned out the lights. In fact, someone turned out the lights in all of our eyes and left behind only a dull hopelessness.

One memory I have of my brother is an incident that relates to his beautiful color. My sister and I caught him at the age of eight years old standing in the bathtub vigorously scrubbing his body with a bristle brush. What was troubling about this scene was the smell of watered down bleach emanating from the tub. He was trying to scrub off his color or at least make his skin tone lighter so the kids at school would stop calling him names. *The cultural message that Black was an unacceptable color was very powerful, and to this day my brother resents the color of his skin and that of his son who looks like him.* Our father constantly reminded us of how our family members often mistreated each other partly due their color or education. This is referred to as internalized oppression. As the oral historian for his generation he knew the full story of how the family had been split apart because of skin color. It was very important to our father that his children understood that we originated from a proud, educated Negro family.

This was his way of trying to explain away the sting of others' stupidity and prejudice.

The Catholic school we attended was our Soweto. Blacks went out one door and Whites the other and it was located near the railroad tracks that literally divided the Black community from the White. One thing is for certain; those years spent at this Catholic school taught us, tenacity, perseverance, defiance, and the purity of hatred, in addition to our academic education. My experience of this hatred did not begin until I was in seventh grade, when all hell broke loose as the adults would say. Looking back, I remember one incident when the nuns called for the eldest children of all five Black families who were registered and attending this predominately all White school to report to Mother Superior's office. Then, we would often be lined up, from the oldest child to the youngest, and scolded or picked out of a line up by a White student who had been battered. This was often a White student who had been attacked by Black students from the public high school across the street. However, knowing this was little consolation as it only required one such student to point at any of us to cause expulsion. Luckily that did not happen, but the terror of being in such a line up remained with us all our lives.

It was not uncommon for leaflets to be passed out after mass that declared in writing how the so called niggers disgraced the church. There was one priest who did not stand for this type of behavior and said so from the pulpit. He was ridiculed as a race traitor and asked to move to our side of the tracks since he loved us so much. He would bring the horrid letters he received from the White community to mass and make them part of his sermon. I can still hear him saying, "Love thy neighbor as you would love thy self." His bravery did not stop the children from calling us names. I remember running home crying about being called a nigger and tar baby. My father told all of us to learn how to walk past and not respond. He believed they would stop their taunting and harassment, but it did not stop them. It continued to the point when I had to fight back. I cannot begin to say how often I was suspended for my behavior, while the White children involved would be exonerated. Was it because of the darkness of my skin? I could not help but noticed how the light skinned Blacks were only reprimanded and sent back to class. Each time I was suspended I would ask my aunt for her help getting me back into school. I feared that if I asked my father he would listen to the school officials' side and beat me severely as a result.

Internalized Oppression

Internalized oppression occurs when an oppressed group comes to use the methods of the oppressor against members of their group. For example, sometimes members of marginalized groups hold an oppressive view toward their own group, or start to believe in the negative stereotypes perpetuated against their group. My father's desire for us to be knowledgeable and proud of our ethnic background was overshadowed by the negative perceptions held within parts of the surrounding Black and White communities. His stated hopes for us were incongruent with what was happening in our environment. Leary (2005, p. 149) supports this belief:

"What happens to us, and to our children, when we are told by our parents that we can be, do and have anything we want, that we are smart, strong and able, while at the same time we are accosted daily with sounds, images and experiences that tell us otherwise?"

Classism

Classism is any form of prejudice or oppression against individuals who are perceived as being from a lower, less educated social class or from a higher socioeconomic status within a class society. The Black societal community dominated our lives. The Blacks who acknowledged these groups, I believe, saw themselves as lesser, by letting certain individuals dictate through collective action, who to socialize with and who would be deemed acceptable by specific groups in the community. This behavior was what Leary (2005, p.16) describes as an intergenerational reminder of "how slaves were divided in many different respects; masters distinguished the house slave from the field slave, the mulatto from the darker-skinned slave, etc." From one interview with my father, I learned that my great-great-grandmother was purchased from another White slaveholder at the age of eleven years old. She was brought to the new slave owners' home to take care of their own children. When my great-great-grandmother became a mother her children were forbidden from playing with the 'quarter' children. The name was given to the children because of where they had to live on the plantation. My father described Black families living in slave quarters as 'quarter' people. It was another way of distinguishing oneself from the slaves who worked in the fields versus those who lived in the slave owner's house. My great-grandfather only played with his sisters, brothers and the White slaveholders' children.

I will never forget an incident from when I was in the third grade when I brought home a school friend from public school to meet my mother. This friend was much taller than I and had a honey colored complexion with long hair that she always wore parted in the middle with two braids. I remember that on this day my friend was wearing a pretty dress. My father came home from work unexpectedly and I introduced her to him. She spoke very politely to both my father and my mother. Yet, after she left to go home, my father roughly spun me around by the arm and with a hateful looking face, he said, "You are never to bring that girl to this house again." I was shocked and in tears, not knowing why he did not like her. 36 years later, while sitting in a circle with a descendant of the slave holder of our family I heard my father speak and say the words 'quarter' people. Later I asked him what he meant when he used these words. He told me those words referred to people who lived in the slave quarters and did not know how to speak or take care of themselves properly. Our conversation mentally took me back to the day my friend came home with me from school. It cleared the mystery up as to why my father told me not to bring this friend back. I remember my school friend used words such as 'dis' 'dat' and 'dos' (this, that, those) and 'flo' for floor and 'sto' for store. She spoke the same way my father heard Blacks who had been raised in the old slave quarters speak. Her form of communication made him believe she was uncouth and would be a bad influence. This old practice of separating blacks from one another still exists to this day. It is the epitome of internalized oppression

The general community rule for acceptance into a particular class was determined by attendance at what were deemed the right schools, the color of your skin, the parents' education and occupations; and the texture of one's hair. This last element was referred to as 'good hair'. Having 'good hair' meant it looked and felt like White people's hair or lacked the kinks often found in Black hair. My father put his foot down on all of it, especially on the idea of 'good hair'; he declared that we were to never say those words in his home, because there was no such thing. Nevertheless, community values took precedence over his rules. Even he had class issues, as stated earlier, if I brought anyone home who spoke, dressed, or behaved like a 'quarter' person he would tell me not to bring them back. The only thing that brought my partial acceptance into the community was my education, because I attended a private rather than a public school. Private schools were valued and known for their high regard for discipline and success rate in college preparatory. Many Black students who attended Catholic schools were accepted into high ranking universities and colleges.

However, my father's place of employment classified us, according to the community societal ladder, as a blue collar and lower middle class family. My father worked at Chrysler. Although my father considered the darkness of my skin to be beautiful, this color also caused me the most pain. It was double jeopardy because my hair was not considered to be smooth and silky by my community's standard; its kinky, thickly curled nature and the dark brown color of my skin did not rank high on the perceived societal ladder. I often thought about hiding out for the rest of my life, because I hated myself and no wonder after hearing my father's claims that, "you never going to amount to nothing when you grow up;" and "all you girls are good for is cleaning," along with "you girls are nothing but trash." This was also the salutation we received from the neighbors, but it was the most hurtful when it came from our father. I believe this is why men tried or succeeded in molesting me. *I truly believed I was unworthy for anything else. Each episode was an out of body experience for me.* These dreaded community values overrode whatever my father had to say to us about being proud of the beauty found in our race. What I did know was that someone had forgotten to inform the Black and White communities, as well as some of our extended family.

What really made this pervasive community disease of classism and internalized oppression consciously humiliating happened when

I was fifteen. My favorite cousin called and asked if I would attend a house party with him. It was in an exclusive part of town called Palmer Woods. I immediately said no, because I knew my kind would not be accepted there. *I realize as I write this how much I had bought into his way of thinking.* He said, "Don't worry about that, it's one of our cousins. I was impressed, because I did not know we had cousins who lived in that affluent area. I dressed in my best, since this was the first time I would see them. After my cousin picked me up, he shared what he knew about them. This cousin had a very fair complexion, with greenish gray eyes. He attended Catholic school, but he and his family were economically poor. When we arrived and knocked on the door, I saw this other cousin of ours for the first time. She too was very light, with long hair, and attended Cass Technical High School, which at the time was considered one of the ten top schools in the nation. I was so excited about meeting her that I did not acknowledge the look on her face when she saw me, we were cousins after all. She asked both of us to come downstairs and have a glass of punch. A few minutes later, she asked my cousin who accompanied me to come upstairs. I was astonished at how these cousins lived compared to us. He returned with a scowl on his face saying we had to leave. I asked why and when we returned to the car he said with tears in his voice, "They thought you were too dark and asked that I take you back home, but said that I could return." I asked, "How could that be since we are cousins?" I thought all of our cousins would be like him, kind, loving and caring. After that incident my cousin never went back. His willingness to protect my feelings and demonstrate his loyalty meant a great deal to me.

CHAPTER SIX

RETRIBUTION

*Freedom is never voluntarily given by the oppressor, it must
be demanded by the oppressed.*

Dr. Martin Luther King Jr.

The issue of discrimination and color had no boundaries, what was happening in the Black community was carried over from slavery times. A lot of the behavior I was subjected to was 'old South' as my father would say, telling us not to pay any attention. He also told us many times how we could be whatever we wanted to be in life. It was hard to pay attention to this message, because we had to face discrimination at school, among the White people and in the Black community every day. Dr. King had a similar experience. As cited by Carson (2000, p.3) the message Dr. King Jr. heard from his mother:

My mother confronted the age-old problem of the Negro parent in America: how to explain discrimination and segregation to a small child. She taught me that I should feel a sense of "somebodiness: but that on the other hand I had to go out and face a system that stared me in the face every day saying you are 'less than,' you are not equal to.

This message was introduced to my siblings and I after our mother died. It was then that our father immediately removed us from public school and enrolled us in Catholic School and scouting. Our father had heard that boy scouts and girl scouts offered the best afterschool programs for teaching discipline and developing leaders. Girl scouting is one of my best memories from those dark days. This experience was like the calm found within the eye of a storm. It was at this time I learned the value of teamwork and accomplishment. The following is a personal experience published in the Girl Scout Totem Council's brochure when I was awarded the 2004 Woman of Distinction Award. As a girl scout, I remember finishing a project that involved building a portion of a fort out of Popsicle sticks. I finished my portion before the other scouts and tried to give it to our Scout Leader. She smiled and said, "You are not finished until your team is finished." At the time, I felt rejected and thought I had done something wrong. However, the impact of her statement remains with me to this day and can be found in the organization I lead which is comprised of departmental teams who work within the context of a larger team. Scouting provided me with my first experience of team work and leadership.

By the time I had reached the eighth grade the nuns had labeled me as a troublemaker. I had difficulty turning the other cheek. Yet, I must admit it felt good to do something. There are three incidents that really stand out for me that took place during this awful, but educational period of my life.

At our Catholic school we received our religious training from the Jesuits. The Jesuits were considered to be the intellectuals and oftentimes the rebels of the priesthood. According to the 1997 *Catholic Encyclopedia* taken from the internet, Jesuits were educators, scholars and missionaries throughout the world. Through their missions, parishes and educational institutions, the Jesuits live out a global commitment to the service of faith and promotion of justice. It is the latter that endeared me to one Jesuit in particular who was French and took on the racism and hatred practiced in our school. He stood up and fought for us, even though he received death threats and disrespect during Mass. He provided guidance to the older students and those nuns who believed like he did in justice and equality for all. Receiving religious training from this group of individuals left you wanting more. It was his encouragement that made me attend the 1963 freedom march led by Dr. King Jr. and Aretha Franklin's father. He was willing to share the good, the bad and the ugly historical facts about the Catholic Church. Yet we received our academic instruction from the nuns.

The Thorn in my Side

Our eighth grade nun stood 5 feet 11 inches if not 6 feet tall and walked with a cane. She belonged to the Immaculate Heart of Mary denomination, which was a group considered to be excellent educators and very strict. This nun openly told our class that she did not appreciate having us (Black students) in her classroom. Believe it or not, we thought it was funny at first and made jokes about it on the way home. Little did we know that our education on racism was going to be up close and personal.

In the eighth grade, there were a total of eight Black students who were divided up equally between two classrooms. We were considered the largest cohort for the school at the time with 44 students who eventually graduated. The next memorable incident involves my interactions with her and the lessons I learned.

Reprisal

This brings me to the second incident. After math exercises our eighth grade teacher's usual routine was to have students go to the board and demonstrate what they had learned. On this day, she called on one of the White students, as always. She made it very clear to us that she believed that Blacks were incapable of understanding higher levels of math. She could have been right about me as an individual but not about my entire group. That day, the White student apparently did not know the answer to the problem she had on the board. One Black female student did know the correct answer and raised her hand to indicate to our teacher that she could solve the math problem on the board. The nun grew very red in the face and called on her. This nun was known among our classmates for humiliating us whenever she could, but this was one time she could not, because this particular student was one of the smartest kids in the room and was almost as tall as the nun. This girl learned early on not to have this nun's anger turned on her. Instead she chose to demonstrate her knowledge in silence and on paper, through her homework assignments or her in-class written work. I can only guess that the nun did not want others to know how intelligent this student was compared to Whites in the class, since this would also make this student appear better than them. *How smart was this student? She later became the first Black valedictorian to graduate from our school.* That day she found her voice by correcting the White student's error. The nun became enraged and took my friend's head in both hands banged it against the Blackboard three times. We were in shock and my friend, whose parents were my Godparents, was on the floor stunned. None of us had ever seen any nun commit such a violent act in a classroom. Yes, they would use rulers to hit our hands or have us hold stacks of books in each hand with our arms straight out until we were uncomfortable, but never this kind of blatant violence.

My friend went home and told her mother what had happened, and they both returned that afternoon to see Mother Superior. Our classroom teacher was surprised to hear that my friend and her mother were there. My godmother came to our class to ask if anyone had seen what happened. She met deathly silence from us and even the White students were afraid to respond. The nun was called to Mother Superior's office, but before my friend's mother left the classroom, she asked us if anyone had seen the nun touch her daughter. Everyone except me said no in unison; *I remember their response almost sounded like a song*, and then she left. What happened next has been imprinted on my mind since that day. As cited by Coretta Scott King (1967, p.43) Dr. King Jr. once said, "Our nettlesome task is to discover how to organize our strength into compelling power" (King as cited by Coretta Scott King, 1967, p. 43). Soon after, the nun and my friend's mother returned to our classroom with my friend and Mother Superior. It was time for me to muster the strength to tell the truth. My friend's mother told the class she was taking her daughter to the clinic to have her head examined by a doctor. Then, she asked again if anyone had seen what had happened to her daughter. The room was deathly silent. The mother turned to the solemn faces of Mother Superior and the nun in question, then turned back to the class and asked us one last time if any of us had seen what happened. We continued to remain silent. What happened next shocked even me. Just as my friend's mother turned to leave the room, I called out her name, spoke as rapidly as possible and told my friend's mother what I had seen. I thought the room was silent before, but it did not come close to the deafening silence that followed my outburst. The nun and Mother Superior said nothing to me, they just left the room. My classmates turned to me and said "You are going to get it now." I knew I was in for some type of punishment, but I did not know what form it was going to take. Yet I did know that this nun was known for finding vengeance through cruelty and humiliation. For example, one time a biracial classmate of mine who was a mixture of American Indian and Black, but who was referred to as Black, and who also had some physical difficulty, needed to go to the restroom. When he raised his hand for permission, she made him state why he needed to go and then made him stand in place until he urinated on himself. The class was frightened and embarrassed for him. The nun scolded him and made him clean it up. He cried the entire time. Telling this story brings back the memory of how the White students were just as afraid as the students of color. Although none of them were directly mistreated they were just as traumatized by these experiences as we were.

After seeing our visitors out the door, the nun returned, walking loudly with her heavy cane into the silent classroom. Next, she asked us all to turn to the English assignment in our books and began walking up the aisle opposite my desk, checking to make sure everyone was turning to the page she requested, or so I thought. Her behavior falsely led me to believe she was not going to address the issue. I thought I had done the right thing after all by telling the truth. This thought was crushed when her cane unexpectedly slammed down near my left hand. I remember her saying, "I see you are left-handed. I want you to write with your right hand from now on and if I see you writing with your left hand I will hit it with this cane." I was scared and devastated by her fury. Then, for the next several weeks, I tried to write with my right hand, but all my papers came back with D's and F's and frankly, I was more afraid of my father than of her. I knew that if I brought a report card home with any D's or F's, I would be severely and physically punished. Recognizing there was little choice, I returned to writing with my left hand, but tried to hide this fact. One day she caught me and instead of hitting me with her cane as promised, I was made to stay in during recess. She asked me to write 50 times, with my right hand only, that I would not write with my left hand. Throughout this silent writing exercise, I periodically looked up to see her sitting at her desk glaring at me and getting redder in the face. She finally exploded and said, "Stop writing and get up. You see those lights above you?" *They were the old fashioned low overhead lights that hung from the ceiling.* "I want you to get up on that desk and swing from those lights. You and your people are no better than the monkeys found in the jungle." *As I mentally review this incident, I notice how my body responds; my shoulders and neck muscles are tightening with rage. How is it possible that I can still feel the same level of intense emotion now?* I lost it and began screaming at her from the top of my lungs, which brought in the lay teacher from next door. *What I fantasized about doing was jumping on top of her while she sat at her desk taking off her cowl.* I was immediately taken to Mother Superior's office and suspended. As I write this story, I realize that my reaction was probably exactly what she wanted to provoke.

Was my suspension actually punishment for breaking the silence? I am convinced that telling my friend's mother what had actually happened to her daughter in our class that day led to my suspension. There were so many cruel and punitive messages I received during this period of my life. Messages like the color of my skin was unacceptable to some of the nuns and priests at my school, and that breaking the ranks by speaking up when silence was demanded would not be tolerated. The most important message I received was there no one to protect the Black students against the blatantly racist name calling and the violence directed against us. This included my father. For example, one day we were late for school because the alarm did not go off. My father was also late for work. When he dropped us off at school, I remember begging him to come inside and explain to the nun what had happened. He interpreted my fear as an exaggeration and said no. I remember he replied, "Whoever heard of a nun lying, or acting in the way you describe?" This was during the same period of time when I had been deemed a liar by his friend and that is how he always saw me. The nun humiliated me like my fellow student, only I was forced to write "I will not be late again" 100 times with my right hand. It was also during this time that I began to break out in hives and display other physical ailments such as migraine headaches and stomach cramps. I feel certain that these symptoms were caused by the horrendously stressful conditions in that nun's classroom. Later in life I often wondered if these ailments also expressed a subconscious desire to return to the safety of the hospital. Throughout my marriage I experienced a return of these same physical ailments. *Could these ailments be considered physical reactions to trauma? One other thought has come to me also; I notice that during this incident my behavior was no longer that of a victim.*

When I returned to school a week later with my aunt in tow, after being suspended for verbally threatening the nun, I learned that something had happened to my classroom nun, because there was a lay teacher who had taken her place. We were told she would be taking our nun's place for the rest of the school year. The class was ecstatic speculated that she must have had one of her episodes in the convent. She never returned and we always wondered what happened to her. All I know is that my prayers were answered. *Thank you God!!*

Discovering Courage

The third incident happened after school, when all the juniors and seniors were getting ready for the homecoming parade. All the Black students had volunteered to help make the tissue paper flowers for the floats at a White classmate's home. There were two White students a male and a female, who were close friends with me and my Black friends. They met us at the student's house who was hosting the flower-making party. While we were there a group of boys who attended the public high school across from the Catholic school entered the basement. At the time, we thought nothing of their presence and continued making flowers for the upcoming dance. This assumption turned out to be a mistake. Within thirty minutes these boys began calling us niggers and telling us that we needed to go back to our side of the tracks where we belonged. When our White friends came to our defense, they called them 'nigger lovers'. Our White classmate's mother heard the noise and immediately asked us to leave. Our White friends were upset and told her that we did not cause the disturbance, that it was the other youths who had just arrived to the flower-making party. Nevertheless, our classmate's mother was adamant that we all leave, including the boys who had started the verbal assault. The Black males left first with their White friend. The Black females, including myself, along with our White friend took a little longer in leaving because our White friend wanted to see if we could get a ride home since it was dark outside. The owners of the home would not let our friend use their phone. Then, when we went outside, an awful sight greeted us. Those boys from the public school were beating up our White male friend and our cowardly Black friends were running down the street. I remembered feeling shocked and angry about them leaving our friend who stood up for us earlier. After those boys kicked our White male friend for the last time, they turned their attention on us and asked our White female friend to approach them. We were afraid they were going to do to her what they had done to our other friend and so we put her behind us. Then, one of the boys went to their car and retrieved an object, we heard a sliding sound. My immediate thought was, "My God! Is it a zip gun?" Zip guns were often handmade from parts taken from other guns. We were unable to see what they had taken out of their car, but my imagination went wild with fear. Our White friend ran down the street knocking on doors for help. Houses were very close together in this district. In the distance we could hear the occupants of one home turn up the volume on their television or radio. I picked up a large tree limb lying next to me. As the boys approached us, I looked at my frightened Black friend and knew without speaking that we would do everything we could to protect each other and our White friend. I was preparing for a fight, even though we did not know what they had taken out of their car. One thing was for sure we were not going to let them do to her what they had done to our White male friend, who was still moaning on the ground. *Even now I feel the cold hand of fear in my chest.* We could hear a car screeching in the distance and our White friend ran back towards us. It was her terminally ill mother who was dying of cancer, coming to get us. She drove the car between the boys and us and then motioned for all of us to get in the car. We were saved that night. *Our two White friends and terminally ill mother made me see that there was goodness among Whites. Our friend's mother died only four weeks after this incident.* That night was unforgettable and frightening for all of us. We went to the police department the next day to report the incident. Everyone in my community said that some of the policemen who worked in that department also belonged to the John Birch Society, a group that was similar to the Ku Klux Klan. It was not surprising that they dismissed our complaint. If a White teenager had registered a similar complaint there would have been hell to pay in our neighborhood.

My friend's mother demonstrated through her actions why a "caring adult" is considered an important element of the 40 developmental assets researched by the Search Institute. The Search Institute is a global leader and partner for many organizations that want to know how to help kids succeed. The Search Institute's work is helping to develop caring adults create environments where young people can thrive. The learning for me was in recognizing that even in the midst of so much hatred there were people like the Jesuit priest, my friend and her mother, who believed in justice. The Black community was not the only target. The Jewish community was another group that was targeted by the John Birch Society and the Klan. Sometimes late at night looking out of my window, I would try and remember a time when our community had no race riots, a time when the Big Four police squad did not terrorize the young boys in the neighborhood and a time when a person did not have to feel fearful when going to the store in the dark. Martin Luther King Jr. as cited by Coretta Scott King (1967, p. 73) says it best:

Violence as a way of achieving racial justice is both impractical and immoral. It is impractical because it is a descending spiral ending in destruction for all. It is immoral because it seeks to humiliate the opponent rather than win his understanding; it seeks to annihilate rather than to convert. Violence is immoral because it thrives on hatred rather than love. It destroys community and makes brotherhood impossible. It leaves society in monologue rather than dialogue. Violence ends by defeating itself. It creates bitterness in the survivors and brutality in the destroyers.

Victim No More

By the time I was sixteen I had run away from home. I had been severely beaten because of a lie told to my father by his friend, the man we called uncle. What happened next was totally unexpected. One night, my siblings and I were sitting at the kitchen table playing cards when our father came through the side door in a terrible rage, and even more frightening, directed his anger at me. I was afraid of my father's fury. When he knocked me to the floor I recall asking him what I had done and he said I had it coming for what I said about his friend's daughter. *My stomach is cramping and I am breaking out in hives as I tell this tale. This is one of my darkest moments.* I did not know what he was talking about, but he struck me again. I pleaded with him to stop. I said, "Whatever he told you it was a lie." He hit me again while telling me that I was the liar. My God! When he hit me that time I knew he would kill me if I did not get out of that house. I managed to get the table between us and asked, "What did he say to you, at least tell me that much?" The story was that I had told some students at a public school near the downtown area that his friend's daughter was pregnant and married, a girl who was the same age as me. I knew this was false because I kept to myself most of the time. I also knew all of the kids on our street who attended public school and we rarely spoke to each other. All I could think about in that moment was why did my father's friend lie about me? What did he want from my father? This family knew how my father valued his integrity and used the lie as a way to make him feel guilty about my supposed wrong doing. My father's friend had access to my father's car, checking account and retail credit card. *I did not find out that night what this man was after until I was in college when my sister told me it involved the daughter in this family and getting her marriage annulled and an abortion.*

I managed to run out of the house and into the street screaming. I kneeled in the middle of the road hoping a car would come and kill me. I could not take one more mental and emotional cruelty or incident of sexual harassment. It was the first and only time in my life that I wanted to die. I got up and ran across the street to the man who told my father's friend what he supposedly learned from me about this man's daughter. He took one look at my bloody, tear-streaked face and asked me who I was. This man who was responsible for causing all of this pain did not even recognize me as the young teenage girl who lived across the street from his house. I asked him to call my father and tell him that I had not been the person to give him this information. Although he called, my father refused to believe him and that only made me wonder again what my father's friend wanted from him. I returned home beaten, swollen, feeling helpless and very much the victim.

The next morning I received the worst blow when my father asked me to go across the street to his friend's house and apologize. I went over there alright and told him and his wife what I thought about their lie. When I left their home, I knew that the fallout from my visit would be much worse even than what had happened the night before. This is when I decided to run away. I left immediately and went to a friend's house where I stayed for awhile. It was my next youngest sister who found me and begged me to return home. It took a few more weeks away from the chaos before I decided to return.

It was not until I was in college that I found out from my sister the truth behind this episode. She had discovered a letter sent to our father from his friend's family members who scolded him for financially helping this friend. The letter revealed that the daughter of my father's friend had in fact been pregnant and married at sixteen, but I did not know that at the time. Her parents had needed money to pay for her illegal abortion and they wanted my father to help them with the money. What better way to make me the scapegoat than to claim I was spreading lies about his daughter's situation. They felt that they needed to cover up the truth from the rest of the community and did so by saying she had the flu; even I had believed that lie. When I later learned that my father helped to pay for the abortion out of guilt it brought back the moment of defeat and anger.

The Unintentional Mentor

During my short time as a runaway, I stayed at my friend's home, but still attended school each day. It was difficult to concentrate on any of my studies or assignments, so I would doodle on my papers. It was all I could manage to do. The nuns would usually take my drawings and tear them up. Yet there was one person who saw these simple drawings as a bargaining chip to get me to participate in his class, my English teacher. He wanted me to turn in my assignments, so he struck a deal. He pointed to the blackboard at the back of the room and said if I turned in my papers at the end of class each day, he would give me a box of colored chalk and I could draw whatever I wanted. I did turn in my English assignments because drawing was not only one of my outlets it was my passion; drawing allowed me to describe how I felt inside. I stayed after school that day and created a mural of two basketball players who were sitting side by side on a bench, waiting for their turn to play. One player stared off into the distance, while the other sat with a towel draped around his neck looking down. It took three days to complete.

My English teacher was surprised by the mural and brought in other teachers to see it as well. This small gesture helped my self-esteem and brought back my pride. My teacher demonstrated how a "caring adult" could make a difference in an at-risk youth's life. Even though neither of us were consciously aware of what was happening this exchange engendered hope. I think that this is when I decided it was time to return home. It was also when I decided to attend college. The wait for my freedom took two long years. This teacher was my first mentor, who steered me in many directions. I became the first Black layout editor for my senior yearbook. He was there when I was denied entry into Wayne State University and coached me through the application process for Eastern Michigan University, where I was accepted.

Rediscovering Joy

In spite of the abusive experiences there were some joyous times during these adolescent years, such as the Civil Rights March and another wonderful event. Prior to running away, in March of my sixteenth year, my father gave me a sweet sixteen party. He worked very hard to orchestrate a large sweet sixteen or coming out birthday party celebration on my behalf. This celebration was very much like those put on in the old slave aristocratic south. At the time, however I only understood one thing, that I was the belle of the ball that evening. Over one hundred people came to celebrate this special event with me. *From this memory I realize how angry I was at my father most of the time, but not on that night.* I remember my father standing tall and proud; of me and the turn out. It was a great moment. I wore a beautiful dress with a wide band around the waist. Wearing this wonderful dress filled me with joy and I pictured myself as a princess at a ball. Every boy who attended asked me to dance. It was obvious that my father felt good about the event because he even allowed my boyfriend to drive me home. This was unusual for my father to do and when he gave the nod to my boyfriend allowing him permission to take me home, it made the night all the more special for me. This all took place before I ran away from home. *It is remarkable how things can turn bad so fast.*

Another similarly joyous occasion occurred three months later when I was formally presented at a debutante ball which came at the end of a twelve month period of preparation. Before you can be presented to society, you have to take classes in how to become a proper lady. Even though this time was stressful, I still felt special and visible. *That is an interesting thought about being visible, when did I become invisible and to whom?* My feelings of invisibility were found in my internal and sometime external fight to be the oldest child. My eighteen months away from the family seemed to take away the privilege of being the oldest and it felt like a constant battle to reclaim this position.

Even my parents struggled with this duality between my rightful position and the second oldest girl's place in line. My father constantly explained to my siblings that I had the right to do certain things because I was the oldest. Although he also struggled to accept my role as the oldest child, and I often found myself frustrated and confused with the lack of clarity about what was expected of me. Visiting relatives would ask if my sister was the oldest, which caused me to wonder what it was about my sister's behavior that prompted them to ask this question. As an adult, I did ask this question out loud only to hear my relatives respond that they did not know why they thought this. *Even now, I feel tormented with wondering why people still ask the question, even though my sister is deceased. Why do I still care?* This internal torment leads me to believe there was a reason for people to think I was the second born. This internal anguish made me look at my own behavior. There must have been something they saw for them to think I was younger. The bigger question is why should I care? *Because feeling anguish about birth order is still within me.* I now believe it is because my father always made reference to my birth order when he wanted me to do something or take on more responsibility. *Internalized messages from our parents have a way of haunting one worse than a ghost.* Trying to deal with other people's expectations of me and not knowing what was involved, caused me to feel a great deal of anxiety. I was so afraid all the time, thinking that someone was going to find me out. I was also afraid to be too joyful. *Is this when I first noticed being fearful of joy?* No, the fear of too much joy came after my mother died. It seemed as though every time joy entered my life something would come right behind it and take that good feeling away. As I shared earlier, before I could make my first appearance at a formal social event in public, I was required to take etiquette lessons. This is what it took to become a debutante. The lessons were supposed to be a positive educational experience, but taught me a few unexpected lessons as well. It was a time when class distinction once again reared its ugly head in my life. This challenge came in the form of a five-way test that considered only five aspects related to a young woman: her hair type, skin color, parents' jobs, neighborhood, and education level. As mentioned earlier these things were definitely considered important by the young women in my group. The first two criteria were determined by observation. The next two pieces of personal information were obtained during our genteel studies when the young women would ask each other where their parents went to high school and/or college to determine not only what part of town they were from, but precisely what class they belonged to. The next question that always followed the first was what does your father do for a living? *As a Rotarian, I just wish I had known the four-way test back then to reply those inquiries asking: Is it [what you are asking about] the truth, is it fair, is it beneficial for all, and will it help promote fellowship?* Instead, these young women's behavior only fueled my anger and brought back the old feelings of shame.

After fighting Whites for my rights, here I was watching Blacks act as though they were White. It is a fact, as Russell, Wilson, and Hall (1992) state, the color complex has long been considered unmentionable, and has been called the last taboo among African Americans (p. 2). This complex also affects the attitudes of many in the African-American intellectual community. Russell et al state: "The complex even includes attitudes about hair texture, nose shape, and eye color. The 'color complex' is a psychological fixation about color and features that led Blacks to discriminate against each other." (Russell et al, 1992, p. 2)

Nevertheless, on the evening of my debut I let their undisguised contempt cause me to fear making my appearance before the audience of parents and friends. When my name was called the others had to push me out on the stage. I regained my composure and walked down the steps to take the hand of my escort who whispered in my ear, "You look better than you think you do." I was scared and ashamed of having to be pushed out on the stage, but his kind statement calmed me. I managed to get through the waltz with my head held high and felt thankful when it was over.

Making the Transition

Going away to college was my way out. Thanks to our father's constant mantra, "You better plan on going to college or find yourself a job because you are not staying here after you turn eighteen." I found out later that he did not actually mean what he said because after his two oldest of children were in college he still had the two youngest children at home, even after they had graduated from high school. My brother and youngest sister did not leave until they were nineteen, one by enlisting in the army and the other through marriage. He had me believing I would be kicked out once I was eighteen, so I began planning how I would leave on my terms. *Could this be considered expanding my horizons and taking fate into my own hands?*

Because I had been inspired by my English teacher, I wanted to go to college and become an art teacher. Even though he was there for me several times during high school, it took me a long time to understand that he saw my true worth. *It just came to me that I needed to see my own true worth, instead of looking for it outside of myself.* Later he came to my rescue yet again when he helped me apply for acceptance at Eastern Michigan University. I was accepted, and never had the chance to tell him thank you. I truly believe in divine assistance and that God and the spirit of my mother had sent this teacher to save me. I do know his intervention gave me something I thought I had lost-hope.

CHAPTER SEVEN

A COMMUNITY AT WAR

I refuse to accept the view that mankind
is so tragically bound to the starless midnight of racism and war
that the bright daybreak of peace and brotherhood can never
become a reality.
I believe that unarmed truth and unconditional love will have the
final word.

Dr. Martin Luther King Jr.

Reclaiming Personal Power

It was June of 1967 and I had graduated from high school. It should have been a happy day, but for some odd reason my father appeared to be in a strange mood. After graduation exercises we went straight home. I do not know what I was expecting, but I thought a small gift or family party was well warranted. I had not only graduated on time, but many of my acquaintances who lived in the community were either pregnant, had dropped out of school, or were behind academically while I was on my way to college. Only a few of us had been accepted into a university. It was a day to rejoice! So why did my father appear to be angry at me? I found out many years later.

At one point during his final two years of life, I read portions of this work to my father, including my description of my high-school graduation. With tears in his eyes he had this to say about that day, "I came to realize that my oldest child was no longer my baby and would be eventually going to college and I was not emotionally or mentally ready to lose you yet." In this moment I noticed myself letting go of the old rage I still harbored toward him. Simultaneously, I noticed the tension in my neck and stomach subsiding. I realized it was time to learn to accept him unconditionally and hope he would someday do the same with me.

I spent most of the summer trying to get hired to raise money for college. This was a difficult task because I was short, small in stature, and looked underage. One of my father's older sisters, who lived in Ann Arbor, managed to get me a job at St. Joseph Mercy Hospital, as a nurse's aide. She also generously made room for me to live with her at her home during my first two years at school. I was scheduled to start my new job during the first week of August. Four days before I was supposed to leave for my new job in Ann Arbor, thirty miles away, the city of Detroit erupted in a riot. It is important to provide a little background to illustrate what lead to such devastation and the current consequences of upheaval in Detroit's infrastructure, with its limited growth economy, lack of employment and one third of all inner city homes condemned.

By 1967, disillusionment had replaced exhilaration and many proponents of social justice had lost motivation to fight for civil rights. Following Dr. King Jr.'s march in 1963, the earlier elation began to erode and community's anger was slowly turning into rage. Why? Due to corrupt lending practices and misguided urban renewal many of Detroit's Black residents lacked adequate housing. Detroit had held the highest homeownership rate among Black people in the nation, but during this period urban renewal projects bulldozed some Black neighborhoods to make way for freeway construction. In order to construct Interstate 75, entire neighborhoods were demolished, displacing most residents into high-rise low-income project housing or already-crowded neighborhoods. The focus of the Black communities' concern was the loss of an area called Black Bottom. This was a popular, much loved Detroit neighborhood where many Blacks would gather to socialize at restaurants, nightclubs and theaters and worship at churches. The destruction of this neighborhood resulted in racial tensions due to the loss of community as well as the loss of housing. Additionally, corrupt lending practices by financial institutions, such as red-lining, restricted the areas where Blacks could live and own property. This meant that in addition to deed restrictions in local communities, Blacks were denied the ability to move to many neighborhoods, including most of the Detroit suburbs. Many homes that were privately owned were bought on land contract at high interest rates and with very short foreclosure schedules. Blacks were trapped and confined to often undesirable areas that were insufficient to hold the displaced population. According to Hersey's (1967) article in *Time Magazine*, by 1967 the neighborhood around 12th Street had a population density that was twice the city average. Black schools in the city were overcrowded and underfunded. In the 1960s, Detroit's total population was shrinking due to White flight although the Black population continued to rapidly increase, due to continued migration from the South. By 1966 Detroit was losing over 20,000 residents a year, most of them White. They left for new jobs, better housing, better city services and better schools in the suburbs. Partially in response to Detroit taxes, Detroit lost 134,000 jobs from 1947 to1963. Between 1946 and 1956, General Motors spent $3.4 billion on new plants, Ford 2.5 billion, and Chrysler $700 million, opening a total of 25 auto plants, all in Detroit's suburbs.

Meanwhile, between 1950 and 1970, Detroit's inner city lost around 240,000 residents. By 1967 the city government was in deep financial trouble as the property tax base dropped. Whites could escape the problems of Detroit, but Blacks were denied loans and, in many cases, the chance to purchase homes in the suburbs.

In 1967, the Detroit Police Department was predominantly White and only 5% Black. Among the Black residents of Detroit the Department's Big Four or Tactical Squads, each made up of four police officers, had a reputation for harassment and brutality. Officers verbally degraded youths, and those that could not produce proper identification were often arrested or worse. My twelve year old brother was one of those individuals. Several questionable shootings and beatings of Blacks by officers were reported by the local press in the years preceding 1967. After the riot, a Detroit Free Press survey cited in the *Time Magazine* article 12th Street Riot (Hersey, 1967) revealed that Detroit residents reported police brutality as the number one problem they faced in the period leading up to the riot. My eyewitness account of what happened in July 1967 during what was to became known as the infamous Detroit riot.

The Detroit Riot

It began as a hot muggy evening and I went to say goodbye to a dear friend before leaving for Eastern Michigan University. I had promised to come and spend the night with her before I left for Ann Arbor. Our parents were out of town together and my siblings were at home happy that I was gone as well. We were sitting on her front porch when we heard what we thought were firecrackers going off near Twelfth Street. *The skin on the back of my neck suddenly feels clammy just as it did on that hot humid evening.* My father's oldest sister lived on the corner of Euclid and Twelfth, near Claremont where the afterhours bar, the Blind Pig, was located. Detroit police raided the bar that night, and sparked the riot. It would be three days before I saw my sisters and brother again.

My friend and I were caught in the middle of all this chaos. We woke up at eight o'clock the following morning to hear people driving down the street laughing and screaming. I looked out the window and saw three men carrying bottles with rags sticking out of them running towards Lynnwood Avenue. I remember laughing with surprise because the sight seemed so bizarre. The world had gone crazy that day.

Suddenly, two blocks over, the local gas station blew up taking out the five surrounding brick homes. We rushed to put on our clothes to go help any survivors. Luckily, many people had gone to work already. Once we were outside I looked down the street to where my father's oldest sister lived and saw a wall of fire. Twelfth Street was entirely up in flames and the paint store on Lynnwood Street was also on fire. The fire trucks were trying to get through, but people were throwing stones. Finally, one man came out of his house with a rifle and shot it into the air saying if another person threw a stone he was going to shoot them. I remember thinking, "My God! What is going on? Are we at war?" As my friend and I looked at the corner gas station near her home, there was an explosion at the paint store on the opposite corner that knocked us to the ground. This is when we came to the realization we were really in danger because the gas station two houses away from her home was also on fire. The man next door started watering down his roof. There was so much smoke, fire, and mayhem that at first we did not know what to do. We ran to help the people where the first gas station had blown up. We kept asking each other, "Where are the police?" We were surrounded by flames and fear.

In the meantime, unbeknownst to us, my father and her mother were trying to get back into Detroit. The bridge that led to my family home had been raised to prevent any looters from getting near Dearborn or other predominantly White areas. It was comforting to know my siblings were away from most of the horror. As for the question about the whereabouts of the police, rumor had it they were protecting the White neighborhoods. Watching a troop of armed, all White national guardsmen marching down our neighborhood streets was the scariest sight. There has been some speculation that the deployment of troops incited more violence during the riot. It is true that National Guard troops were engaged in firefights with locals. These fights resulted in deaths both to locals and the troops. Tanks and machine guns were used in the effort to keep the peace. Film footage and photos shown internationally were of a city on fire, with tanks and combat troops in firefights in the streets, sealing Detroit's reputation for decades to come. This was not mentioned in any of the local papers. They invaded our community with their fear. Did they truly intend to maintain peace or just forcefully demand order? I only know this invasion brought more violence and destruction to my world. Because of this experience I can truly empathize with people whose countries have been invaded.

Although I did not know it, by that evening, I was in shock. I was sitting on my friend's porch trying to make sense of this new world when I realized I had not eaten anything all day. The electricity, phone and water were out, but I thought there might be some food at the corner store that appeared to still be operating. Due to my condition of shock, I was unaware of the guardsman at the bottom of the walkway and also of the fact that we were temporarily living under Marshall Law with an enforced curfew. As I was walking towards the corner store a young guardsman pointed his rifle at me and ordered me to stop. I did not think he was speaking to me because I was unarmed. There was sniper fire going on and off in the distance throughout the evening which seemed unreal. I remember asking myself in a dream like state, "How could there be sniper fire here, this is the city for goodness sake?" Nevertheless, for the first time in my life I had a gun in my face and it was in the hands of a frightened White boy. If I had taken one more step I believe he would have shot me. I went back and sat on the porch step visibly shaken looking out at the destruction. *To this day the smell of stale smoke will sometimes bring back the screaming in my head from that time.*

I remember sitting there watching a Black man down at the corner. He was sitting on the sidewalk crying and talking about losing his cat in a house fire. His home was one of those that went up in flames earlier, after the first gas station exploded. The man who had shot his rifle into the air earlier in the day had scared the looters away from the gas station next to us, and the firemen were able to put out the fire and save my friend's home. That was the last time we saw any fire fighters after the crew saved my friend's and neighbors' homes. Apparently, they were asked to decline any incoming calls for help because it was considered too dangerous to enter our neighborhoods. This also explains why there was so much smoke and so many fires burning unchecked. My friend had to make me get up from the porch to find safety.

Later, during the night, a sniper managed to get up on her roof. We heard a guardsman say "Shoot out that light," referring to the street light next to her house. My father who managed to get through the barricade the morning of the second day shared his memories of that day:

As I was looking down from the window that evening a White state trooper was telling one of the seven troopers below to shoot out the light to stop the snipers from seeing them. I believe the snipers were Vietnam vets, because of the way the battle was fought throughout the night. There was no way ordinary citizens could fight with that kind of precision and using those tactical maneuvers. You had to have been in the service to fight the way they did. It was guerilla warfare.

The guardsman and state troopers could not find the snipers. This, I believe, caused the governor to call for the army to come and stop the riot. I tried to make sense of what was happening. The national guardsmen had fired at the light and missed twice. Finally the sniper said "I'll get it" and shot out the light. Quickly following this, the National Guard began shooting at the house. We were inside screaming, "We are inside! Stop for God's sake we are inside!" *As I tell this part of the story I am sobbing out loud, because I realize now just how close we came to becoming casualties of war. I must stop and take a pause.*

Once the national guardsmen began shooting, we heard the sniper run across the roof. We figured he knew the neighborhood, because the guardsmen were unable to catch him. Only someone who knew my friend's neighborhood would know about the short cuts through the alleys. Later that night the guardsmen repeated their actions and shot into another home, only this time they killed a four year old child. *I find I have to stop and pause again because of how difficult it is to bring back these old memories or should I say the horrors of the past.*

At this point the war was only beginning since the guardsmen were having trouble keeping both Black and White looters out of the stores. By the second day, when it looked like the riots were getting closer to the White neighborhoods, the army was called in to help. Now this was a day to remember, tanks rolling down our city streets to be used against us and they did use them that day on several apartment buildings. The army received some misinformation that a particular apartment building was harboring snipers. People were running away and screaming a warning that the army was planning to shoot into an apartment building near Twelfth Street. I thought they were mistaken because this was not Vietnam, and then I heard the loud boom. I guess I was wrong. After this horrendous event, tensions ran high between the White army and the Black community causing smaller riots, protests, and sit-ins. The new generation was rebelling and held very strong beliefs. Many times these beliefs led to violence.

It is important to read a White person's perspective of the riot. This perspective provides a clear picture of how divided the Blacks and Whites were at that time. This account was written by a White woman who felt compelled to comment on the riot, yet was not in the rioting area. This is a known fact, because Detroit was under Marshall Law and all White people were asked not to enter the affected areas. This account was retrieved from the internet in 2004. It is taken from a newspaper article featuring a description of the riot given by a woman named Sophie who resided outside the inner city of Detroit:

One of the worst riots in United States history was in Detroit, Michigan. On July 23, 1967, police raided an illegal bar in the city. They arrested some people. Before the police left a crowd had gathered outside the bar. This led to protest. The same night that small protest turned into mobs of people looting buildings, burning, and committing random acts of violence. Thousands of people were out in the streets. Hundreds of properties were damaged. Some believe this happened because of a lack of police intervention. But the police at the time said they did not want to send in police. In past riots police were sent in early and this sparked more violence and destruction. So the Detroit city police held back on sending in police.

The rioting continued through the night. By morning it had gotten out of control. Police were helpless against the mobs of people protesting, burning and looting. There were fights in the streets, and many people were injured or arrested. The civil disturbance turned into a race riot. Different racial groups were fighting Whites and only burnt Black businesses or homes and same for Blacks. On the second night of the riot Blacks came from other parts of the city to help fight with other Blacks. The city was divided into sections of Black and White. The section that was a mixture was stuck between the two, where some people joined in the riot with people of the same race. Others would not join, which many times led to their house or business being burned. They were also subject to physical violence. All the hate from the past that people thought was gone came back out into the open. Blacks were at a lower standard. Racism raged through the streets. On the third day army troops were brought into the city. This was the first time anything other than police had to be used in a riot. The troops and police used tear gas and night sticks. Dogs were brought in to keep people controlled, but nothing would stop the people who felt strongly about getting rid of the other group. The police combined with army troops, finally gained control of the thousands of people raging through the city. When the riot was over fourteen square miles of urban neighborhoods had been destroyed. Forty-three people had been killed, seven thousand arrested, one thousand three hundred buildings destroyed, and two thousand seven hundred businesses looted. The riot was heard on radios and TVs across the country (Sauter, 1968).

This newspaper account of the event fails to mention the National Guard being sent into our neighborhoods a full day before the army. To this day when I smell the scent of stale smoke it is accompanied by the memory of death and destruction followed by the sound of screaming in my head. When this happens I must find a calm place to quiet the screaming. In therapy, I later came to realize that these are my own screams I am hearing in my head. I returned home from the war, wearing a once bright yellow shell that was now black and feeling totally exhausted from three days of living in constant fear and terror. I will never forget those three horrific days. I still have an occasional nightmare about the riot or smell smoke where there is none. I am sure there are many of us who were at the epicenter of the riot who are still experiencing episodes of post-traumatic stress disorder from those unforgettable days. What many forget is that this was the second damaging race riot in Detroit's history. The first occurred in 1943, was also instigated by Whites and left over forty people dead.

Remarkably, on the fourth day, I left for my new job in Ann Arbor, one day later than planned. *I still wonder how it was possible that the horrors of three days appeared not to touch me at the time.* The nursing staff was surprised to see me. They thought no one could get in or out of Detroit. However, I had been determined to leave after I made sure my sisters and brother were safe. Yet, I also wondered how I was able to bounce back from such a horrific experience as though nothing happened. This behavior proved to be a consistent pattern of how I would deal with other traumatic incidents in the future. I had apparently learned how to unconsciously remove myself from the situation in order to function according to societal norms.

CHAPTER EIGHT

THE COLLEGE YEARS

We will discover the nature of our particular genius when we stop trying to conform to our own or to other people's models, learn to be ourselves, and allow our natural channel to open.

Shakti Gawain

This particular phase of my life was enlightening because of the experiences I had through higher education that paved the way to leadership. It was the end of the 1960s, the beginning of the aftermath of the civil rights movement from the 1950s leading up to the assassination of Dr. Martin Luther King Jr., in 1968. The impact, upon hearing of the death of Dr. King, was far-reaching and in some cities and on some college campuses violence erupted. On our campus you could hear loud crying and screaming in the distance. The Black students were either angry or inconsolable. I was inconsolable, not comprehending how this could have come to pass. Part of my sorrow, as I think back on this sad day came from the feeling of hopelessness. Yet I also remember a moment that brought back the hope I felt at the march in Detroit. This feeling of inner peace came through a single act of kindness.

On the evening of Dr. King's death, the Black students at my school decided to hold a candlelight vigil. This was to be a silent march through campus holding our candles high to commemorate a great man. As the African-American students silently walked in a single file, I remembered looking back to see how long the line stretched. I was astonished when I saw it was at least half a mile in length. One White student approached two of us to ask if she and her friend could join in the line with their candles. It was unexpected. We said yes without thinking about what the other African-American students might say. This must have been a signal for other White students waiting in the darkness because we were quickly joined by at least ten others and the line grew even longer. It was a beautiful and sad sight to see. A single silent line of lit candles held high in the dark. Even the wind was silent. Dr. King's death ignited a fire in our hearts and we all wanted to see some changes on our campus.

At this time, I was a member of the Black Student Association that was responsible for what followed. We submitted a list of demands to the administration that identified some changes we wanted to see. We asked that Eastern Michigan University offer Black history, hire more Black faculty; and purchase books on our culture for the library. When it appeared that our demands were going unheard there were student demonstrations. These demonstrations were overshadowed in the press by larger demonstrations at the University of Michigan's campus ten miles down the road. Nevertheless, we were determined to get our demands met. The evening that the Black Student Association took over a building on campus, I was scheduled to work, but joined the other students as soon as my shift ended at the hospital. We barricaded the door to prevent any administrators from getting in the next morning.

The energy around this event was highly charged and we all felt giddy with power for pulling something like this off, or so we thought.

The next morning when the administrators could not get inside the building the police were called. The males were the leaders of our group and they stated that the campus administration had to meet the demands given to them earlier. The official response was swift. The police were able to wedge the doors of the building open wide enough for their German shepherd dogs to get in. The dogs immediately corralled us in the hallway. I was caught, wedged between a water fountain and the wall, and I was not going anywhere. The police broke through the barricade and arrested our leaders. I thought I was going to be arrested as well, but I had a guardian angel among the administrators who watched over me and came to my aid in the midst of the chaos.

The Second Mentor

My second mentor was one of the first Black administrators at Eastern Michigan University. We all believed that he and two other Black men benefited from the civil rights movement and the beginning of Affirmative Action. Eastern Michigan University is located in Ypsilanti, often referred to as Ypsitucky. This was because there were so many Southerners from Kentucky, Alabama and Florida who moved in the area to work at the Ford plant; along with the three brothers Klu, Klux, & Klan, who were probably there already.

This particular administrator adopted me after an incident at the University's Art Department involving the all White faculty. I was an art major and looking forward to having the freedom to draw and paint. Since I had never received any formal training in the visual arts I was unprepared for the formality and expense of the field. I was paying my way through school, but was unable to keep up with the expense of the art supplies. I was told by other African-American art students that the department really discouraged Blacks from being in this field and that all I could expect to receive for grades were C's and D's. However, I was not going to let their attitude deter me. *As I write this, I am wondering if my defiance and tenacity were demonstrating resilient behavior.* I did go back to one of my art professors with a request to drop his course since I was unable to purchase the supplies required to complete the assigned work. He refused to sign my request saying I had to find a way to get those supplies and stay in his class. All I could think about was the possibility of failing his class, which would place me on probation. I did not know what to do. I went to the Dean of the art department to ask him to intervene on my behalf, as I was still within the allowed time frame for dropping this particular course. He also declined my request. His refusal left me stunned. Why would they want me to fail this course? There was very little I could do to purchase the supplies, short of stealing them from the art store. Silently, I cried inside as I desperately tried to figure out how I could maintain my academic standing.

This situation led me to the newly hired Black administrator in charge of admissions. I told him my story and he simply handed me a pink slip and said "Just show this document to your professor and everything will be alright." He was right. It did remedy the situation, but not without making both the Dean my art instructor irate. The art instructor stated in front of the class that I better not take another course from him, but later that summer I did just that, and passed! From that time on, during the four years I attended Eastern Michigan University, I was one of the five students this Black administrator took under his wing. He became our mentor and coach throughout those four years.

Racism and oppression were very much a part of my college experience. After the silent demonstration on campus following the death of Dr. King, the University did not allow any other student demonstrations. However, one day while waiting in the dining hall for a friend of mine, I noticed a curious parade. It was a single file line of individuals dressed in all white. It was an unbelievable sight. It was the Klu Klux Klan carrying torches and coming to the only dorm that was predominantly filled with Black students. We all looked upon this sight in horror. The Klan members turned to face us on command, then set up a wooden cross in front of the dorm and set it on fire. How do you fight such hatred? One way was to refuse to let it get us down. We had every right to attend University as any White student. There were many White students who were also appalled and who felt ashamed by this sight and stood by our sides. It was encouraging to see White individuals who were willing to sacrifice themselves to protect the rights of non-Whites. Their actions kept my hope alive.

Founding of Hamilo and Company

Founding Hamilo and Company, a performing arts group, was one of the ways I fought the oppressive environment in Ypsilanti. It was during my second year at Eastern Michigan. Two other dance students joined with me and volunteered to form a performing arts group called Hamilo and Company. This troupe was comprised of youth ranging in age from seven to seventeen years. The performing arts company offered dance, poetry, staging, and acting to disadvantaged Black students in the community. Today these students would be referred to as African-American students at-risk.

This was the first volunteer activity I participated in while attending college and working at St. Joseph Mercy Hospital. My colleagues and I managed to raise $30,000 with the help of my mentor who taught us how to write a grant and make a presentation to funders. We used these funds to take seventeen disadvantaged youths and five adults to New York City. We took this trip during the time I was pledging Sigma Gamma Rho and was President of the line. The line is a term that refers to sorority pledges who are required to walk in a single file at all times. While writing this chapter, I also see the emerging pattern of my current working behaviors. *I wonder if I was still running away by unintentionally becoming an overachiever.*

By the time of our trip to New York, we had lost one of the founding members of Hamilo to marriage. My remaining colleague and friend helped me to introduce these seventeen youths to other performing art groups such as the Negro Ensemble Company, and we saw Ozzie Davis and Rudy Dee perform. We also had the opportunity to tour the United Nations, and perform on the Staten Island ferry. The Hamilo and Company performing arts group was the beginning of a lifetime of volunteering and community activism. I identified with the needs of these youth because I once was one of them.

Confronting Jim Crow

It was then that the ugliness of racism and hated infiltrated Hamilo and Company. It was after we returned from New York that this particular incident occurred. Even though the evidence and rules of Jim Crow were all around me, without the signs it was easy to break them.

Because I let my guard down, the Hamilo troupe was exposed to blatant acts of racism. We had just completed a very successful performance at Southwestern High School. My colleague and I wanted to reward our young performers with a meal before returning to Ypsilanti. I thought it would be safe to go to a restaurant in Melvindale, a sundown town five miles outside my former home in Southwest Detroit. Sundown towns was a term used to refer to places where Blacks were required to be off the streets by 6:00 p.m. or suffer harassment from local police. What I failed to remember about Melvindale was that during all those years my father took us there as children, he never took us inside to eat and always purchased our ice cream at the drive-up window.

When we entered the restaurant I immediately knew something was wrong. Maybe it was the sudden silence that happened when we sat down at five of their tables. The waitress refused to serve us until I went up to her and confronted her with the fact that I had seen her attend to two other patrons who arrived after us. She turned away and returned to take our orders. What happened next will stay with me always. Our salads were served without tomatoes, causing two of our youths to inquire about them. The waitress walked away, but returned with the tomatoes in her hand and practically threw them in their bowls. I asked everyone to stop eating, because I was afraid that they could have put something poisonous in their salads. I asked everyone to return to the cars. The owner of the restaurant approached me in a rage demanding that we pay for the orders. I left a penny.

Starting the performing arts troupe was my rite of passage, and while some of my memories are painful, Hamilo and Company reminds me of the joyous and hopeful parts of my past. After graduating from Eastern Michigan University, I was hesitant about teaching and planned to remain at St. Joseph Hospital for another year, until a phone call I received at work propelled me into my first teaching job. Apparently, someone from my alma mater had referred me to Fellrath Middle School as a good candidate for the new art teacher they would be hiring. I often wondered if this referral was a going away present from my mentor who had also moved on to a new position in Newport News, Virginia.

This high ranking Black administrator was the mentor and coach I introduced earlier. He was responsible for admissions and often referred to by some Black students as the spook who sat by the door. This phrase was actually stolen from a title of a book written by Sam Greenlee (1969). Greenlee's story portrays a White firm who is looking to fulfill the new Affirmative Action mandate by hiring an African American and then having them sit near the door so he or she can be readily seen. However in using this reference to my mentor my peers were dead wrong. My mentor's complete focus was directed toward helping his five wards to be successful. He believed in our abilities and skills and taught us to believe in them as well. He promised to stay at the University until each of us had graduated which was a sacrifice for him, because his wife lived in Newport News, Virginia. However, he kept his promise and waited until we all graduated before leaving his post.

CHAPTER NINE

PARENTING AS A LEADER

Being the mother of a Black child it ain't no easy thing
you got to call on Jesus and listen to the angels sing.

Mona Lake Jones, 1993

My marriage began with each partner fantasizing what we thought the union should look like without showing each other the script. For me, marriage was supposed to be the answer to my feelings of loneliness and joylessness. I had hoped he would provide me with feelings of overwhelming happiness and joy. This notion came from foolishly believing friends, sorority sisters, family members; and other women who told me stories about their wonderful honeymoons. I believed in the magic of romance novels; and also from watching other couples who held hands and whispered to one another when they took walks together. My unwillingness to let the past go kept me from what I most wanted, intimacy. I had few if any female role models who could tell me whether what I thought was missing was realistic or not. It was not until after my divorce that I learned that we are each the gatekeepers to our own souls and happiness. Embodying old messages prevented my sisters and I from being open and honest with our mates.

Physically, my body held onto the memories of all the assaults, expressed through tension headaches, severe stomach cramps, hives, and an eating disorder. The eating disorder started in my teens when I would go days without eating, subsisting purely on water, soda, or milk. It was my belief that men would not want a skinny girl and would leave me alone. I was wrong. The eating disorder continued during college and followed me into my marriage. When I graduated from college I weighed less than ninety five pounds and still thought I looked too fat.

After graduation, starting a new chapter was the most important thing in my life. A year later I married my college boyfriend and twelve months after that became pregnant with my first child. During this time I was teaching sixth to eighth graders art. Yet, my self-esteem was very low. *After resurfacing the memory of all the assaults, I wonder if they had anything to do with my low sex drive and inability to participate in the act. I just know that sex became one of our many challenges as a couple.* It was as though the light was unable to penetrate the shield of armor I had adopted as perceived protection during the emotionally scarring experiences of my earlier years. Yet this armor kept out both the negative and the positive experiences in my life. The sexual traumas experienced in my past interfered in my married life at an unconscious level and made it difficult for me to be intimate or trusting in the relationship. Our marriage never stood a chance and after 20 years we finally divorced.

A New Life Chapter

Before moving to the Seattle area, I nearly died immediately following the birth of my second child. The caesarean procedure required was difficult, and left me with Septicemia, a type of bacterial blood poisoning, throughout my system along with multiple infections. The doctors came to my bedside and told me that they were unable to determine what was causing this massive infection. Because I was a former employee of the hospital, the doctors wanted me to know the truth. The doctors then informed me that if they were unable to determine which antibiotic to use to fight the infection I could die. I was placed on an ice mattress for seven days to keep my fever below one hundred and five degrees. My body convulsed with grand mal seizures. Once my temperature fell below one hundred and one degrees I was allowed to breast feed my baby. At that time I also requested that the nurses walk me to the nursery. Receiving assistance from the nurses who got me up and walking helped me cheat death.

A short six months after this incident, we moved to a new city. In doing so, I left all of my support systems behind and had no one to talk to when episodes of post-traumatic stress syndrome would emerge. In the past, whenever my sisters or I went through moments of terror, desolation and depression we were there to talk each other through it. We each knew how the ghosts from our past kept us vigilant and wary for the safety of our daughters; we were all so afraid that a man would take advantage of them. During this time after our move to a new city my husband labeled my constant depression, unexplained illnesses, complaints about my weight, and perpetual irritability as strange. What was happening to me was just as unclear and strange to me as my behavior must have appeared to my husband. During this time my children gave me moments of joy but I would frequently holler and scream at my husband out of frustration. I felt that he was not doing his job, which was to keep me happy. It was during one of my husband's trips away from home that it hit me and realized it was my own responsibility to make myself happy. This thought came on the heels of a session I had with a counselor at Eastside Mental Health. My depression was interfering with how I interacted with my children and husband. Since my sisters were not there to talk me through it, I looked for help. During this period of my life I sought out different religious communities looking for spiritual guidance, to help me take charge of my life. I later learned that this guidance was already dwelling within.

During my single session with the counselor, I came to acknowledge that I was in charge of my own happiness. This new message did not prevent the bouts of depression or desolation, but did reenergize my determination to reinvent myself and get back in the game. This was about the same time my father sent my youngest sister and her daughter to live with me. He knew we needed each other. My older sister remained in Detroit. She was also struggling in her marriage and fighting bouts of depression. It was our legacy, but my sister helped reenergize me. With my renewed energy I opened a dance and aerobic exercise studio in the Bellevue area. This business allowed me to become more financially independent, and to pay for my children's Montessori education and daycare. They were with me most of the time due to their father's business trips. However, my old struggles with an eating disorder also reemerged at this time. What helped me through this period was remembering the strength and tenacity of my father's mother.

Nancy Josephine Davis-Harden

John. Gardner (1995) writes, "Leaders often exhibit the wounds from their early losses and have tenacity, even ruthlessness that may prove difficult for others to comprehend." He also cites Winston Churchill's comments taken from Winston's father John's biography:

"Famous men are usually the product of an unhappy childhood. The stern compression of circumstances, the twinge of adversity, the spur of slights and taunts in early years are needed to evoke that ruthless fixity of purpose and tenacious mother-wit without which great actions are seldom accomplished (p. 33)." John Gardner (1990) also states, "Leaders come in many forms, with many styles and diverse qualities. There are quiet leaders, and leaders one can hear in the next country; some find their strength in eloquence, some in judgment, and some in courage" (p.5). My grandmother modeled courage, tenacity, ruthlessness, and hope, which were qualities she instilled in me during the two years we lived together while I attended college.

My grandmother entered our lives for the first time when my siblings and I were teenagers. My mother tried to bring us together earlier when my siblings were between the ages of four and seven, but we were frightened of our grandmother who was still living in the mental institution. Our grandmother also had difficulty accepting any of her grandchildren because she had not given permission for her children to marry and therefore, in her eyes we were all illegitimate.

Until her death in 1979 at the age of ninety-two Grandmother Nancy was a long-time survivor of violence and trauma. Nancy Williams (2002) a resiliency theorist cites Shuler, Gelberg, and Brown (1994) whose words illuminate my grandmother's ability to survive living in a mental institution for thirty-two years:

"For survivors of violence and trauma, spirituality is a significant ingredient in the healing process for many in that it gives people a sense of connectedness to self and others and an ability to see a larger meaning or purpose to the events of their lives."

Nancy Josephine Davis Harden was one such survivor; an independent free-thinking woman of her time. She fiercely believed in a higher power. Nancy was born in 1887 and grew up in Mt. Pleasant, Florida. My grandmother was the daughter of a slave whose father taught her self-discipline, and the meaning of independence, freedom, and education. He encouraged her to receive educational training at Florida A&M College. She taught in segregated rural schools in Florida and later in Philadelphia.

My grandmother was unable to marry until her mid-thirties because at that time female teachers were not allowed to be married or have children. My father explained, "It was thought that married women took jobs away from men who were trying to provide for their family. It was alright for a single woman to work and make a decent living under certain conditions." These words, taken from the autobiography of Bessie Kidd Best, entitled *Unbeatable Bessie: Biography of Bessie Kidd Best* (Kyle, 1988) corroborate my father's statement:

When Bessie took office, her salary was $2,400 per year, and the Flagstaff Superintendent of Schools was paid exactly double that amount. This was a standard figure for county superintendents' salaries. Statewide in this biennium, thirty-one male grade school superintendents and high school principals averaged $4,691. A lone woman in the same category earned $3,100. The belief system which perpetuated this inequality in pay is the same one which kept married female teachers from teaching in Arizona's public schools: men were the sole breadwinners of the family. Therefore, they were paid what was called the 'living wage', enough to 'take care of' their wives and families without any help from the wife. For this reason, men had to be paid more, because it was assumed that they had more responsibilities. When running for office, Bessie defined herself as widowed rather than divorced because to be a widow suggested that a woman must support herself and any children (as was Bessie's case) and it was easier to explain than divorced status, which was at this time rather uncommon and generally frowned upon.

As this quote explains unless a woman was a widow or unmarried and supporting herself, she was not welcomed in the workforce because it was expected that her husband would provide for her.

My grandmother had suffered a multitude of childhood traumas under the regimen of the Southern societal norms and also as an adult, as a teacher in the segregated South and North. Yet she was determined to be independent, free and as she would often state, a "God-fearing woman." When Grandmother Nancy's husband died, leaving her with five children and no income, Nancy knew it was important to find work to feed and house her children.

This is her story told to me when we lived together from 1967 until 1969 while I attended college:

After my husband died in 1932, I later disguised myself as a man so I could work at the (car) plant in Dearborn. I was returning home one evening on the trolley car, when a White man accused me of smoking a cigar in the car, it quickly turned into a scuffle with the conductor stopping the car at my normal stop. He apparently asked for assistance from a White policeman nearby, who separated me from the White man. He dragged me from the car with me screaming and telling him I did not start it. It was then that the policeman noticed I was a woman dressed as a man. He took me to the stationhouse. I told them I had five children at home without a father who needed me. They refused to listen. The next morning I was taken to Ypsilanti State Hospital where I remained until my second youngest child Sarah who was five when I left had me released thirty three years later.

This story is what led me to ask my father for his eye-witness recollection thirty five years later.

When this event occurred my father was ten years old. He was standing across the street watching the police remove his mother from the trolley. When I interviewed him in March 2004, his mother had been decreased for twenty five years. I shared my grandmother's story with him and could still hear the emotions of anger, shame, humiliation and later forgiveness in his voice. Below is an excerpt of that interview:

Researcher: Daddy what do you remember of that incident?

Dad: I was ten years old at the time and it was my job to walk my mother home each evening from the trolley. I will never forget that day. *His eyes were misty with tears.* They said she went crazy and the police had to take her away.

Researcher: Did you believe them?

Dad: Not at first, but later on we did. Baby, what was I suppose to think? The police came with welfare services and placed us all in foster care.

Researcher: Do you believe that now after hearing what grandma told me?

Dad: I believe my mother was a strong woman especially in those times and finding out that she was able to remain sane all those years in Ypsilanti State, I don't know how she was able to do it. It could only have been her faith that got her through that ordeal.

My father revealed what helped my grandmother get through that time was her faith in God and the survival skills she acquired as a child growing up in the rural South.

Through this informal dialogue, my father also learned how his children had been sexually molested and subjected to mental cruelty at the hands of his friends. During our discussion he went through denial, anger, and finally acceptance. We both experienced intense emotion that evening. We cried convulsively in each other's arms. He had to learn to live with guilt and his remorse over the loss of our innocence. I had to learn to live with his sorrow. That evening opened a new door in our relationship. It was the first time we both brought authentic mutual acceptance into our conversation. We both found it unnecessary to guard our thoughts and words. This new element in our relationship led me to realize I could not change my father, but I could accept and love him.

This particular interview with my father was very rewarding and moving. He saw his mother in a different light because he never heard her side of the story until our face-to-face dialogue in March of 2004. In that instant I realized my father had also experienced a traumatized childhood. It was overwhelming to learn that he and his siblings had been placed in foster care with strangers for a year, and then sent from an urban environment to the rural South. Because his grandparents were either former slaves or born just after the civil war exposed him to the standard disciplinary procedures for Blacks in that time period. Since both grandparents learned to adapt through the brutal post-reconstruction era, they taught their children and grandchildren how to survive. Leary describes this well (2005):

> The slave family existed only to serve the master and in order to survive physically, psychologically and socially the slave family developed a system which made survival possible under degrading conditions. The slave society prepared the young to accept exploitation and abuse, to ignore the absence of dignity and respect for themselves as Blacks. The social, emotional and psychological price of this adjustment is well known.

Parental Heritage

My sister who was closest in age and I each had one daughter, while our youngest sister had two. We did not want to see our daughters go through the same experiences we had. The legacy of hope we decided to leave our daughters is one of the values that fuels their independence. Three of these four women are now in their thirties; one is married and three are unmarried, and clearly in no hurry. What verbal and nonverbal messages did we give them? Did we do our job of teaching independence too well? My second sister has three sons and I have one. We wanted to groom our sons to become loving companions and husbands, to help them become the type of men we dreamed of for ourselves. Two of them are happily married and successful. I wish I could take all the credit but it took the dual efforts of both parents to raise the type of children I am so proud of today.

CHAPTER TEN

PROTECTIVE FACTORS

I used to think there would be a blinding flash of light
someday, and then I would be wise and calm and would
know how to cope with everything and my kids would rise up
and call me blessed. Now I see that whatever I'm like, I'm
pretty well stuck with it for life.

Margaret Laurence, *The Fire-Dwellers* (1969)

Let's start with how a leader is defined. According to Gardner (1990), "Leaders perform the function of goal-setting in diverse ways. Some assert a vision of what the group (organization, community and nation) can be at its best; others point us toward solutions to our problems." There are several famous individuals who fit this description and who suffered childhood traumas including Sojourner Truth, Eleanor Roosevelt, Dr. Martin Luther King Jr., and Wangari Maathai. Each of these leaders transcended the crippling impact of childhood traumas to become a broadly recognized leader. Dr. Martin Luther King Jr., Eleanor Roosevelt, Sojourner Truth, and Wangari Maathai dedicated their lives to serving others by shining a light on, and bringing solutions to societal or political problems. These four were not political leaders according to the definition given by Gardener and Burns (1978) who believe that political leaders are motivated by ambition, recognition and the need for power. This may be true of many leaders, but individuals such as Dr. Martin Luther King Jr., Eleanor Roosevelt, Sojourner Truth, and Wangari Maathai have been described as servant-leaders. Greenleaf (1991) states "the servant-leader is servant first." Each of these four notable leaders attracted followers in times of crisis and served the highest priority needs of other people beyond their own, even if it meant their lives or reputations suffered.

Through resilience, all four of these notable individuals overcame their personal challenges to become inspirational or transcendent leaders. Brooks and Goldstein, (2004, p.3) believe that a resilient mindset has these main features:

Feeling in control of one's life

Knowing how to fortify one's 'stress hardiness'

Being empathic

Displaying effective communication and other interpersonal capabilities

Possessing solid problem-solving and decision-making skills

Establishing realistic goals and expectations

Learning from both success and failure

Being a compassionate and contributing member of society

Living a responsible life based on a set of thoughtful values

Feeling special (not self-centered) while helping others to feel the same

My own development shows all but one of these features. The area that still offers challenges is fortifying my stress hardiness. My drive to overachieve oftentimes affects my health and relationships.

These habits materialized during my college years when I worked at the hospital four days a week, while attending college. This should have been enough, but in addition to this I started a performing arts troupe, pledged a sorority and became president of my line all while carrying 14-16 credits a semester. Why I was driven to do so much remains a mystery to me. I stacked my responsibilities one on top of the other, and this mindset became normal. My need to overachieve is still evident today.

My first mentor taught me how to create realistic goals and expectations, but it was my second mentor who created a protective environment for me to learn from my successes and failures, become a compassionate and contributing member of society; live a responsible life based on a set of thoughtful values; and finally, to feel special (not self-centered) while helping others to feel the same.

The protective environment my second mentor created gave me the freedom to control my own life. This freedom took my energy and concern off of my own plight and turned it into having compassion for others who exhibited life experiences similar to my own. This freedom provided my colleagues and me the opportunity to become contributing members in the community outside of our college life. We exhibited this in our performance art troupe comprised of disadvantaged youth who lacked a community center and were dealing with fears about their aspirations meeting a dead end. Co-creating a protective environment for these youth, with the help of my colleagues, brought them a measure of hope. Their accomplishments made us feel special while helping them to feel the same.

Another example of co-creating a protective environment occurred during an interview with a nonfamily member. I conducted some interviews with nonfamily members who were self-identified survivors from abusive situations. These nonfamily interviews were also conducted in a dialogue format. One such conversation was with a White female who shared what happened after her mother's death. She was the eldest of four children. Her family composition was similar to mine, three girls and one boy. Being seventeen and the oldest she believed that she could take care of them all, but in less than a year her father remarried. This new disruption in her life caused her to feel anger towards her father because of her perception that he had somehow replaced her with another woman. Then, their lives were forever changed by an abusive stepmother.

As I listened to her story I found myself remembering how I had also believed I could take care of my siblings after the death of our mother. When my father said he had to take my four year old sister away because I was too young to care for her at age ten, it left me thinking I had failed him. I was unaware that he had little choice but to remove her from our home under the risk of losing us all. Over a period of time I forgot that she existed. I learned later through trauma therapy that apparently my brain had only repressed my memory of her. It took a long time for me to recall the times she returned to our home for visits.

I shared my story with my interviewee including how I took care of my baby sister when my sick mother could no longer use her hands to change my sister's diapers. I also shared how authorities told my father that a ten year old child was too young to be responsible for the care of his youngest child. At the time my father was forced to hire an adult to help, and I thought I had done something wrong. I asked my interviewee if she had believed the same thing. She responded that yes, she had also felt guilty and blame worthy when her father remarried. By using the same informal approach in my interviews as I had with family members, we co-created a trusting environment that led to an open dialogue filled with empathy and mutual sharing. To this day, and suffers from migraine headaches that the medical profession cannot explain or cure. Yet in spite of her physical affliction, she is a successful community leader, who has earned her doctorate and is recognized for her work with vulnerable children and women; an overachiever.

During the period when I was studying applied behavioral science at Leadership Institute of Seattle (LIOS), my third and fourth mentors helped instill me with effective interpersonal communication skills and taught me how to best reach out to the community. Both in school and through the guidance of these mentors I also developed problem-solving and decision-making skills. These two skill sets are incredibly important in the political arena and for effective community development. I learned how to be thoughtfully articulate and responsive, which requires patience and strong listening skills. I learned to be authentic in the moment and show empathy when appropriate. This requires conscious awareness of what is being communicated in the present moment. I learned to paraphrase and repeat back what I hear and also how to ask for needed clarification through the practice of appreciative inquiry. Appreciative inquiry is an approach that allows the researcher to hear another person's experience by asking questions to generate new and affirming conversations. Even in awkward moments, it was important that I learn to co-create a protective environment with potential voters by sharing an open dialogue and lessening any feelings of defensiveness.

Many resiliency researchers believe protective factors such as personal disposition and social responsiveness can bolster self-esteem and build a stronger mindset (Greene, 2002; Goldstein & Brooks, 2005). The many interventions I have received throughout my life are partially responsible for who I have become. Palmer's statement (2005) identifies specific values a child adopts consciously or unconsciously as they learn about life through the experience of relationships. Palmer's book provides the guiding values and beliefs of the Fetzer Institute (2004):

Every person is grounded with an inner source of truth, which is the root from which our capacity for loving and forgiving grows.

(a) Our inner life of mind and spirit is interrelated with our outer life of action and service.

(b) Just as we hold ourselves and others accountable for words and deeds, so also do we hold ourselves and others in our hearts. This is basis for trust and freedom.

(c) The more we refrain from quick judgment and avoid the temptation to solve problems for one another, the more likely we are to learn with and from one another.

(d) Authenticity and integrity are based on respect for diversity.

Creating a protective environment that provides these values and attributes can instill a traumatized child or youth with hope.

Risk-taking skills are another element of leadership that may be developed in a protective environment. Burns (1978) and Gardner (1995) believe risk taking and the willingness to go to great lengths to achieve one's end are qualities that are often exhibited in early childhood. Burns also believes that the ability for risk-taking correlates to an aptitude for learning political prowess. The observations of Burns (1978) and Gardner (1995) identify many of the leadership characteristics found among all the notable leaders studied; leaders who each experienced a traumatized childhood. I have also manifested many of these characteristics, in my work as a public speaker, educator, political activist and international volunteer. These same qualities have served me in my artistic and creative endeavors, my ability for independence and interdependence in relationships, my determination and my spiritual grounding. According to Nancy Williams (2002), finding hope, spirituality and meaning in one's life experiences are some of the resiliency factors seen in survivors. A great example of this is found in the book *Sojourner Truth* by Nell Painter (1996), "Truth would have explained that the force that brought her from the soul murder of slavery into the authority of public advocacy was the power of the Holy Spirit." Greenleaf (1977) believes nothing is meaningful until it is related to the listener's own experience. Dr. Martin Luther King Jr., Eleanor Roosevelt, Sojourner Truth, and Wangari Maathai were four survivors of trauma who became notable leaders. They also shared an ability to tempt others to connect with them after hearing about their experiences. Surely, each of these leaders would ace Greenleaf's (1978) three question test:

(a) Do those served grow as people?
(b) Do they, while being served, become healthier, wiser, freer and more autonomous, more likely themselves to become servants?
(c) What will the effect be on the least privileged in society; will they benefit, or, at least, not be further deprived?

Each of these four leaders in his or her unique way passed this test, as shown through the legacies they left behind.

While exploring the attributes of protective factors, I wondered how each of these individuals, who all experienced traumatic episodes as children, transcended to become leaders. For them to rise above their circumstances to become renowned leaders was a phenomenal accomplishment, considering the painful intensity of episodes in their early lives. Protective factors are also addressed by resiliency theorist, Nancy Williams. She notes that "resilience theory often attempts to seek answers to the question: Why do some children succeed and overcome challenges that adversely affect the development of other children?" Williams (2002) citing Warner and Smith (1992) explains:

Some children receive protection from the negative effects of an outside traumatic event by caring adults or a supportive community, institutions, or a stable family environment.

It was later surmised by several resiliency theorists that children who lacked such protection later had challenges with a sense of future, problem-solving and social skills. Eleanor Roosevelt did receive some of this protection, even though her family's culture was dominated by values concerning class, wealth, and physical beauty. Under the care of her parents Eleanor was subjected to an oppressive environment created by the very people who should have loved and cherished her. Her mother showered her with disappointment for a perceived lack in Eleanor's physical beauty, while Eleanor's father was consumed by addiction. Yet it was her grandmother, although known to be stoic and seemingly uncaring, who realized her granddaughter would be better off receiving a proper education in Europe, for her future and for her protection. This education built Eleanor's faith in herself, required her to adapt and encouraged her social and emotional growth.

These skills are described as internal assets that affect how a child overcomes challenging circumstances.

Greene (2002) citing Bernard (1993) writes:

Protective factors such as adaptation, self-efficacy, spirituality/ social and emotional development and self-actualization are the reasons some children and youth can transcend to become great leaders. By having a strong capacity to form relationships, solve problems, and develop a sense of identity, resilient children and youth are able to plan and hope.

Let's take a look at each of these protective factors:

Adaptation

Adaptive skills can be defined as pumped up coping skills that help to develop the capacity for successfully meeting problems based on an individual's values and purposes. By facing painful memories or current events, developing new attitudes and behaviors an individual learns to distinguish reality from fantasy and resolve internal conflicts. Ronald Heifetz (1994) author of *Leadership without Easy Answers*, focus on adaptive challenges when leading others or making decisions. Heifetz believes that understanding different methods of survival, such as accepting the fact that what may have worked well in the past may not work well in a present situation, can help a leader to better adapt. His strongest message is to remain open-minded. It is also important to know that the internal messages carried inside our heads, originating from parents or caregivers, can become barriers to adaptation. For example, my youngest sister internalized many of the negative messages my father sent and became mentally paralyzed as a result; believing his cruel accusations that she was never going to amount to anything. This became her mantra and created a huge barrier to adaptation in a new environment. When my sister moved from Detroit to Seattle she was literally waiting to fail. Unfortunately, these old tapes limited her professional and personal growth. It was not until later, through coaching and encouragement, that she came to believe in herself and adapt to her new environment.

However, positive parental messages can also directly or indirectly prepare a person to adapt in any environment, especially one of inequality. Parental messaging can help children learn how to adapt in an oppressive environment. My father's positive messages about African American culture and history definitely helped me, and importantly this protective factor is not limited to one particular ethnic group and as noted by Greene (2002), is applicable to any group of people who have experienced oppression.

Self-efficacy

Self-efficacy as defined by Bandura (1977) can help determine how people feel, think, motivate and behave. He believes that individuals are capable of demonstrating behaviors that influence events and eventually affect not only their lives, but the lives of others as well. Many resiliency theorists consider self-efficacy to be one of the protective factors influencing leadership characteristics that will often appear during traumatic times. Other characteristics that show up are insight, independence, relationships, initiative, creativity, humor, and morality. These same characteristics can become a double-edged sword; some of the strengths found in survivors of traumatic childhoods can become obstacles in their adult relationships. Bandura (1977) defines self-efficacy as the means for people to achieve a greater capacity to control personal events. For my siblings and me this characteristic emerged out of a period of inertia. We had been waiting for adults to discover what was happening and come to our rescue, and when this did not occur we took charge of our own safety as best we could. Exhibiting the courage to embrace one's fear lessens feelings of fear and anxiety and minimizes defensive behaviors that can later become obstacles. This behavior also leads to the development of qualities such as courage, insight, determination and persistence. All these attributes contribute to self-efficacy, adding value and furthering tenacity and the ability to self-care. When an individual learns to accept help and find meaning in his or her life through a mentor or coach, he or she begins the process of transcending adversity. (Williams 2002)

Spirituality/Social and Emotional Development

Spirituality is one of the strongest drivers in my life and acts as my internal compass. This protective factor provides me with personal motivation to seek out a higher source of strength to guide me in my life's work. This factor is validated by a statement taken from Everson (1992) who argues, "That the root of all traumas is spiritual abuse, where a young person is cut off from the power that can give him or her life's meaning and purpose" (p. 27). It is my belief in this inner and outer source of strength that helps me to overcome obstacles, make decisions and lead others. According to Nancy Williams (2002, p. 195-215), author of *Surviving Violence: Resiliency in Action at the Micro Level*, this allows individuals who seek ways to change their circumstances to view hardship as an opportunity for personal growth and development. Development of resilience is tied to spirituality and the ability to provide hope and reassurance in the face of distress. It is important that teachers, counselors and parents cultivate, nurture, and nourish the spiritual being within. Citing Brooks & Goldstein's book (2005) entitled *Handbook for Resilience in Children*, Ann R. Conrad

(1999), writes, "The definition of a spiritual person is someone who tries to find a person, thing, or place to overcome their obstacles by searching for something larger than themselves to discover meaning and belonging (p. 29). Spirituality deepens and expands a person's values and perspectives and allows social and emotional maturity to develop. I strongly resonate with the definition of spirituality Maya Angelou (1993) provides in her book, *Wouldn't Take Nothing For My Journey Now.* In it she writes, "Spirit is an invisible force made visible in all life" (p. 33). Similar to Maya Angelou, I believe that Spirit is one in all of us, is universal and ever present. Angelou provides her most significant definition of Spirit (1993, p. 34) when she writes, "It is this belief in a power larger than myself and other than myself which allows me to venture into the unknown and even the unknowable. I cannot separate what I conceive as Spirit from my concept of God. Thus, I believe that God is Spirit." Could this be the Spirit that these notable leaders each called upon many times? *As I ask this question, I look back in my mind's eye and see myself reaching out to this same source during anguishing, happy, and solemn moments.* Spirituality is a significant ingredient in healing and for providing hope. A strong connection to Spirit is also what was missing for leaders such as Hitler, Stalin, and others who chose a path of destruction. Spirituality provides leaders with the ability to see a larger meaning or purpose to one's life. It also provides protection and a way to cope with the trials of everyday life as well as deepening and expanding one's values and perspectives. Dr. Martin Luther King Jr., Sojourner Truth, Wangari Maathai, and Eleanor Roosevelt viewed the adversity in their lives as an opportunity for personal growth and development. One example of Dr. King's spiritual and personal growth and surfaced at the start of the Civil Rights Movement. When one of the organizers of the Montgomery boycott approached him and asked him to participate, he was reluctant at first. This was in part because he did not see himself in the same way as the community. He was described as a man with a commanding voice that demanded your attention. Additionally, he carried himself in a way that appeared polished and intimidating at the same time. Individuals present on the day of the boycott noticed King appear to reach down inside, connect with his inner courage and then step out front. As Frady (2002, p. 35) states, "It was the most dramatic instance yet of Dr. King sharing his mystic capability of leaders of genius, at certain critical moments, to suddenly transmute into someone, something, awesomely larger than their ordinary selves."

Self Actualization

The concept of self actualization was brought to notoriety by Abraham Maslow through his hierarchy of needs theory. Self actualization refers to the final level of human development that may be achieved when all basic, emotional, and mental needs are fulfilled. For example, Dr. Martin Luther King Jr. often received praise from his parents, teachers and a supportive community in his youth and later in his adulthood (Gardner, 1995). He had caring relationships with his parents and grandmother that included positive messages from them as well as from the surrounding community. He was made to feel productive and of value. He managed to consciously and unconsciously self actualize in the face of overwhelming obstacles. One of these obstacles was institutional racism.

Brown (2002) agreed with Blaut (1993) and Miller (1997) that institutional racism presents people of color with a huge obstacle to self-actualization. Institutional racism is reinforced by the practices of White supremacy, which draws an invisible line in the sand. In addition to institutional racism there are other 'isms' that marginalize the lives of people of color. These 'isms' happen when White males or any dominant entity creates an entire social, political, economic, and cultural system. These 'isms' include sexism, classism, and assigning individuals who miss elements of a four-way test to the bottom of the ladder of privilege. Among ethnic and non-ethnic communities alike, these malignant obstacles often dictate how traits such as color, gender, sexual orientation, mental and physical acumen will be valued. This malignancy, which excludes any person deemed different from those on higher rungs of the ladder of privilege, is destructive. They are especially harmful to children and youth of color, because these groups are unable to blend into the dominant culture as easily as some. Individuals from these groups often must fight overwhelming obstacles, including the trials of overcoming traumatic experiences, in order to self-actualize.

Let us explore some of these obstacles that are hurdles for many leaders who are outside of the dominant group.

Internalized Oppression

Roberto Peña (2005) provides an excellent example of internalized oppression in an excerpt taken from *Community and Difference: Teaching, Pluralism, and Social Justice* entitled, *Water Is Clear like Me*:

It was during his childhood when he became conscious of constantly straddling two worlds, one of color and the other White. He was born into a Puerto Rican family where some of his siblings were possibly darker in hue than himself. He states how a childhood friend pointed out this fact by saying: "Look at you—you're so White you squeak. I remember when Eddie said this and I knew at once he was right. I could not go forward and I could not go back."

Pena's feelings of immobilization appear to be a by-product of internalized oppression. This is another insidious disease intentionally or unintentionally sanctioned by national policies and other institutional systems and embedded in our collective psyche. Greene (2002) supports my statement when he writes, "The idea that children must learn to function in two cultural systems applies to diverse children who may experience unequal treatment." The fact of internalized oppression is ever present for children of color who live in a multicultural society dominated by a primary group.

Three of the four identified leaders directly or indirectly experienced institutionalized racism along with some form of internalized oppression during their journeys from childhood to adulthood. Frady (2001) refers to this experience when he describes Dr. Martin Luther King Jr. as an excruciatingly serious child filled with ambition and eagerness for life. It must have been a chilling discovery for King growing up in a middle income Black community, to discover that much of the larger surrounding White society assigned him to a lesser class solely on the basis of his skin color. The trauma for African Americans living in the Southern part of the United States and to some extent those dwelling in the Midwest and on the East Coast is immeasurable and particularly devastating. Yet, King managed to overcome.

Classism within the Black community is another form of internalized oppression that rears its head through the assignment of class distinctions based on one's color, grade of hair, and station in life. The color line in America exists not only between communities of color and the White community, but among its own ranks. Berg (1994) clearly hits the mark when he states:

Race is more problematic. We tend not to realize this because
of the widespread false assumption that race is somehow

biological; but a few moments' reflection should convince us that it is an entirely social construction. For example, there are people who would be considered Black in the United States, colored in South Africa, and White in the Caribbean; there are people who are Native Americans while on the reservation but Black when they leave it. Moreover, the supposedly biological rules of descent are different . . . for different racial groups—one one can be half Asian, but not half Black.

Leary (2005) challenges us to see that one of the obstacles in the Black community is the age old problem of the color line. This challenge attacks from the inside creating a dual world. Peña (2005) shares how his color elicited expectations that required him to act out an unnatural role:

> I grew tired of playing the game, the role, and of acting the silence that I was supposed to be; tired of being nothing, tired of short-circuiting my brain and reacting as others would have me react and acting as I perceived they wanted me to behave. I could no longer repress my emotions and humanity to appear White and as a reflection of what others thought I should be.

Pena's reflection on his emotional state and lack of mental well-being expresses the feelings of many who live inside in two or more cultures.

Gender Issues

Being a woman in a leadership position has been both rewarding and difficult. Berg (1994) speaks eloquently about gender issues when he writes, "if we reduce gender contradictions to class we will have a hard time explaining why women's oppression persists across changing modes of production (Labor markets)."

The female gender, regardless of ethnic ancestry, oftentimes finds it harder to develop the leader within when having to fend off the other obstacles mentioned earlier. My experience as a female within the global culture, let alone as a woman of color has been more than demanding. When I think about the traumas that Sojourner Truth, Wangari Maathai, and Eleanor Roosevelt suffered I wonder how these women increased their capacity to actualize themselves as leaders. This question then spurs me to rethink how each of the four identified leaders approached the call to higher attainment. In many instances these leaders spoke to their higher being to guide them, whether externally or internally.

For example, Painter (1996) identifies how Sojourner's sanctification in her belief of God's constant support released her from the crippling conviction that she was nothing.

This realization helped transform her from an evangelist into an anti-slavery feminist. This new found strength was evident when she spoke out in trepidation in the speech *Ain't I a Woman* against those who stood in the way of women's rights. Sojourner believed that women's rights would empower women in many ways: the right to higher wages, the right to inheritance, the right to hold public office, the right to attend institutions of higher learning, the right to have access to professional careers and the right to have custody of their children. Sojourner Truth probably also recognized that her fight would pave the way for her people to receive Civil Rights. Her fight also paved the way for others to instill themselves with many of her qualities and values.

CHAPTER ELEVEN

REASON FOR HOPE

I refuse to accept the view that mankind
is so tragically bound to the starless midnight of racism and war
that the bright daybreak of peace and brotherhood can never
become a reality.
I believe that unarmed truth and unconditional love will have the
final word.

Dr. Martin Luther King Jr.

The first person aside from family members to enter my life as a caring adult was my high school English teacher. He was the first adult who nourished and nurtured my potential as an artist and encouraged my development in this arena. Even though it was difficult to see his reason for pushing me forward, I listened and grew. It was his insistence, belief in my abilities, and certainty that I would be accepted into college even though the nuns believed otherwise that kept me moving forward. What would have happened if that teacher had missed seeing my inner spirit? What happens when a traumatized child or youth receives little or no positive interventions such as support from a caring community or mentor?

Alice Miller (1998) made the connection between the devastating effects of childhood corporal punishment and adult violence. Miller identifies what maltreatment and childhood abuse without intervention can produce. She makes the following statement on her website:

I found it logical that a child beaten often and deprived of loving physical contact would quickly pick up the language of violence. For him or her, this language became the only effective means of communication available. However, when I began to illustrate my thesis by drawing on the examples of Hitler, Stalin, Mao, Ceaucescu, when I tried to expose the social consequences of child maltreatment, I first encountered strong resistance. Repeatedly I was told, 'I, too, was a battered child, but that didn't make me a criminal.' When I asked these people for details about their childhood, I was always told of a person who made the difference, a sibling, a teacher, a neighbor, just somebody who liked or even loved them but, at least in most cases, was unable to protect them. Yet through his presence this person gave the child a notion of trust and love. (p. 1)

This knowledge is now scientifically proven and in 1998 was finally officially accepted by the American Academy of Pediatrics. (Miller, 1979, p. 2) Brooks and Goldstein (2005, p. 224) also describe child maltreatment as causing depression and intense sadness or irritability that could disrupt concentration, sleep, eating, and energy levels leading to feelings of hopelessness. I can testify to the truth of those findings because I was at a crossroads in my life when my English teacher decided to take me under his wing. If he had missed the opportunity to step in, I could have remained a runaway and lost hope of alleviating my situation. Sometimes one act of kindness is enough to make a difference. Considering how all four children in my family were maltreated and afflicted with various levels of depression, sadness, and feelings of hopelessness it is not surprising that these feelings followed us into adulthood.

Miller (1979) was renowned throughout Europe after she wrote about Hitler's childhood in *For Your Own Good: Hidden Cruelty in Child-Rearing and the Roots of Violence.* Miller's book, written in 1979, portrays abused and silenced children who later become destructive to themselves and to others. Miller believes that Adolf Hitler was such a child. Hitler was a survivor of childhood trauma without any interventions. Heifetz (1994) stated that Hitler "wielded power but did not lead. Hitler played to people's basest needs and fears." (p. 24) Erik Erickson (1963), who wrote *Childhood and Society,* points out how Hitler was constantly mistreated by his alcoholic father, exposed to domestic violence then emotionally abandoned by his mother. As a result he learned only cruelty; how to be obedient and to accept daily punishments with unquestioning compliance. His early years of abuse shaped him to believe that cruelty was the norm. Miller cites Hitler's words as an adult, "It gives us a very special, secret pleasure to see how unaware people are of what is really happening to them" (p. 2) Even with this ability to control and manipulate others, his sheer force of personality, and astonishing ability for organizing and mobilizing, he still fell into periods of depression and withdrawal. (Erickson 1963, p. 329-30)

When there are little or no interventions in a child's traumatic life it shapes who they become as adults. For example, two of the four siblings in our family were maltreated and emotionally abandoned. They were constantly harassed and called cruel names, either in reference to the fact that we had no mother or to the color of their skin. This name calling by other Blacks in reference to skin color came out of collectively unconscious acts of internalized oppression often referred to as the color complex. This constant harassment caused my siblings to internalize these negative statements, and go on to make devastating choices in their teens. As Russell, Wilson, and Hall state in *The Color Complex: the Politics of Skin Color Among African American* (1992, p. 2), "Traditionally, the color complex involved light-skinned Blacks' rejection of Blacks who were darker. The complex even includes attitudes about hair texture, nose shape, and eye color. In short, the color complex is a psychological fixation about color and features that leads Blacks to discriminate against each other."

In addition to the name calling these siblings suffered at school and in our community, all of us were severely beaten by our father, often at the slightness provocation. Even though this was the standard discipline of the day, it left us all with physical, mental and emotional scars. My brother could have easily been one of the people described in Miller's (1998) article, *The Childhood Trauma*, found on her website. On top of the treatment he received at home, my brother was unfairly expelled from Catholic school. This incident followed on the heels of an altercation provoked by White students. After expulsion, he attended a public high school in a community known for its excellent schools. He attended this school for one year before being expelled for inciting a riot. This was in part due to the fact that my brother was a charismatic leader in high school and was able to inspire others to follow his actions. His final placement was in a high school located in a rough area of Detroit. He finally graduated and made an attempt to attend community college. Sadly, but not unexpectedly when my brother brought his first grades home, my father belittled his efforts.

We all craved our father's approval and recognition. If my brother had received any slight encouragement from our father, it might have been the intervention he needed. However, my brother's response to my father's treatment was to drop out of college and join the army. My brother was a survivor of violence and trauma who received very few interventions outside of those provided within his family. He eventually became self-employed, married and fathered six children.

Thankfully, my youngest sister received some interventions in her life after she became pregnant at age 16. In her interview she shared with me that one nun at our school had taken a particular interest in her. This nun coached her with advice about how to graduate on time with her friends by attending school both in the day time and in the evening. This sister managed to graduate from high school on time and with the help of our father also took care of her child. Later, a cousin in the family made it possible for her to acquire a job at a nursing home. These small interventions made a difference in how my sister saw herself. Her self-confidence grew when she left the state to join me; and years later, with a friend, she went on to found a drill team for girls that included her youngest child. Among the four of us, she was the strongest survivor, had the most compassion and showed the kind of forgiving nature we all wanted to emulate.

CHAPTER TWELVE

DEVELOPMENT OF A LEADER

I once was lost but now am found, was blind, but now I see.

Lyric from the song, Amazing Grace

My first conscious brush with leadership was by accident. It came from a conviction to do the right thing and march with Dr. Martin Luther King Jr., in June of 1963. And, as I shared earlier, I disobeyed my father to be at the march that day. My father had been unexpectedly scheduled to work and was unable to find a babysitter for my siblings. He knew how much I had anticipated and prepared for attending this march and half-heartedly had to tell me to stay home with my siblings. Yet once he left the house I felt compelled to find someone to watch them. My strong commitment to reach my goal drove me to override any fear of the punishment I would receive for disobeying, because I knew in my heart the chance to participate in this civil rights march was destiny speaking to me. I look back in amazement at how my participation shaped the person I am today, a person who fights against social injustices, both personally and professionally.

My goals in life were few in my earlier years: attending college, getting married and having children were at the top of the hit parade. However, during college a pattern of behavior began to take shape. I was asked by a fellow student to choreograph some dances for some local economically disadvantaged teens. It started off as a favor and ended up bringing me four years of opportunities; I learned how to negotiate, write grants, and became a leader of a performing arts troupe at the age of nineteen. As I shared earlier, my greatest accomplishment during that time was working in partnership with two of my friends to raise $30,000 to take youth ranging in age from 7 to 17 to New York City and introduce them to the performing arts community. We had been told it could not be done, yet through perseverance and overcoming what seemed to be insurmountable challenges my friends and I made the impossible possible. Even then, the motivation driving me was an overwhelming desire to achieve. Bass (1990) would characterize this as a leader with a strong drive for responsibility and completion of tasks, vigor and persistence in the pursuit of goals, as well as the willingness to accept the consequences (p. 87). I would characterize my behavior as that of a human being who was trying to survive, get along in the world, and find a way to better my conditions. Hall (1994) states, "This struggle to survive and then see a vision for a better existence for ourselves is the innate experience of hope (p. 78)." According to Gilligan (1982), "feminine and masculine perceptions of that seem to develop differently. Girls perceive survival in terms of the preservation of relationships, and communication arises as the means to get along in the world (p. 79)." These statements bring clarity as to why I have felt so driven at different times in my life and also validate my ongoing motivation to teach and act as a role model. My skills were needed in the greater Metropolitan Detroit area and became the springboard for my return. As an educator in the Inkster and Detroit Public School systems, I found it imperative to set an example because I once was just like many of my students. I too battled traumatic abuses and feelings of inner worthlessness, until I found a way to get out and avoid becoming another statistic.

After graduating from college this desire to return to Detroit and teach stemmed from a hope of repaying the gifts that had saved me from embracing the darker side of life after a tumultuous childhood. My early years in the hospital and the eight horrific years afterwards were instrumental in creating my low self-esteem, but were also the breeding ground for perseverance, courage, determination, and strength. My past experiences were most telling with regard to how I operated in groups and my inability to readily access my emotions in the moment. This explains the uncomfortable feelings I experience working with strangers in small groups and how I am more comfortable at leading, because it allows me to facilitate others' interactions. Hall (1995) identifies how interpersonal skills involve the ability to express and manage emotions. He also states that an individual needs to be able to do both in order to elicit cooperation rather than alienation from those we work and relate with in our daily lives (p. 156).

The Darker Side of Myself

I have often wondered how I managed to overcome the downward spiral caused by events in my life. This downward spiral had me heading towards an abyss at an incredible rate of speed. As Hall (1994) states, "Whenever business is bad, when we have a crisis at home, or even when we have to take an examination, these values raise their heads and draw us back (p.82)." As Hall (1994) identifies, my haste to seek security prevented me from "risk taking and the ability to see the truth of anything outside of my own opinions (p. 83)." *As I write this I have the painful realization that my self-interest and attempts to avoid healing most likely laid the foundation for my divorce.* One of the things I was seeking to be released from in my marriage was my husband's controlling behavior, such as his habit of shushing me when I became angry and used foul language. In our marriage, I experienced his behavior no differently than when my father would tell me I had to be with others when I wanted so much to be alone. I had to learn what true courage and compassion looked like before I could emulate these qualities.

Courage and Compassion

On numerous occasions important people have entered my life at the most unexpected moments. It would be difficult not to believe that there is a higher power watching over me, because mentors have always appeared at the most critical points along my path. As I shared earlier, my first mentor was a White English teacher, who entered my life when I was sixteen, the most difficult time of my life. My overwhelming troubles with my father's friend and awful pressures from our surrounding community were preventing me from concentrating on my studies. At the time, I was attending a Catholic School which I found to be strict and overly confining, creating an environment that made it difficult to learn. This teacher however, must have seen a promising student who needed encouragement. He had no direct knowledge of what was going on in my life, yet reached out and intervened.

At the time, many of my school friends considered me a talented artist. I loved to draw, especially when I was sad. Drawing helped me to make sense of the world. I often drew pictures in class, which the nuns did not allow. They would take my drawings away and destroy them. However, my English teacher took a different approach and struck a deal with me. He made me a promise that if I would hand in my English assignment at the end of the day, he would provide me with colored chalk and the entire blackboard at the back of the room to draw on, whenever I wanted. It was this gentleness and authentic caring for my inner child that inspired me to become an art teacher.

What is a Mentor?

Bass (1990) states that mentoring tends to be paternalistic in that it provides a role model for the protégé to follow (Levinson, Darrow, Klein, et al., 1978). Bass went on to say that mentors use their greater knowledge, experience, and status to help their protégés and do more than merely act supportive or give advice (p. 835). Gardner (1990) saw mentors as similar to farmers, who are in a patient partnership with nature, as well as having an eye for the weather and knowing when to cultivate (p. 169). This is exactly the role that Mr. Farmer took in my life. Two years later when I wanted to go to college and the nuns were discouraging me he again showed his belief in my ability to be successful and took the time to assist me with filling out the applications. He also helped me prepare for the SAT exam. Partly because of his intervention, I attended and graduated from Eastern Michigan University, carrying two majors and a minor. I also worked my way through college as a nurse's aide, while dancing and traveling with my performing arts company comprised of youth. My pattern of behavior was that of an overachiever, running away from her past and her thoughts. Murray (1938) cited by Pfeiffer (1991) shares that an individual striving to accomplish something difficult, or to do something for the first time, or win others over, has a high desire to be measured on the basis of achievements and, ". . . loves being measured on the basis of results." (p. 241). I was definitely driven to achieve whatever goal I set for myself, even at the cost of my health.

During college, my second mentor was the first and highest ranking administrator of color. He intervened on my behalf during a racially based incident of discrimination between me and the art department. I came to find out that I was not alone, and that most students of color experienced discrimination in the art department, causing many of them to either change their major or leave school altogether. I chose to stay and fight. This mentor entered my life when I was attempting to drop an art class because I lacked needed funds for art supplies. That same day my art instructor had granted permission for two White students to drop his class. However my art teacher made an example of me by refusing to grant me permission to drop his class, knowing that he could give me a failing grade if I did not turn in the required assignments. On top of this, the Dean of the art department refused to override my instructor's decision. I was irate and decided to fight back. I went to the Registrar's office and found my future mentor, who had the power to override both the dean and the faculty member. After he helped me to successfully drop the class, he became my mentor for the duration of my undergraduate career. He was also instrumental in getting the disadvantaged youths in Hamilo and Company a trip to New York. As Bass (1990) points out, my mentor did more than verbally support my efforts; he coached me how to walk through the political processes of academia, taught me how to network and showed me how to write a proposal.

My mentor from college also helped to build my self-confidence in my ability to start over from the ground up. His coaching helped prepare me to create a new life for myself after I moved to the Seattle area. For the next twenty years I focused on building a new career, which began in the field of health and wellness. In the Seattle area, I started my own dance studio and later continued working in this field, but at a financial institution. These new directions combined my physical attributes, teaching background, and managerial abilities.

Leadership Institute of Seattle (LIOS)

In 1988, I was enrolled at City University earning my Masters in Business and Public Administration. During this period I took a class in leadership and management, not realizing it was part of the LIOS program. It was the first class I had taken that put a primary emphasis on self awareness as a leader. Then, I became a student at LIOS from 1989-1992, and after that a teacher, teaching on the LIOS faculty from the fall of 1991 through 1993. In evaluating my adaption skills, I think my openness and highly participatory involvement in an ever-changing environment was due to my perception of safety and trustworthiness that came from my experiences at Leadership Institute of Seattle (LIOS) Applied Behavioral Science Graduate Program. These experiences speak to my nature to survive in most environments. It was through the ability to control my environment. This probably speaks to my seeking leadership roles or eventually evolving into one.

My involvement at LIOS helped me to rediscover that creative little frightened girl I had forgotten. I believe the adaptive skill was demonstrated in taking risk in the larger group often referred to as 'the community.' It was in this community that I learned how to state how I felt or thought. This was something that I was afraid to do at home with my husband and children, without internally feeling put down, even when it was in jest. I also learned how to be open to feedback, understanding it sometimes came with pain.

Control was another issue for me. When I first joined the LIOS community, I carried a deal of mental baggage. I constantly found myself struggling with internal issues of conformity and control. My training at LIOS taught me to have the courage to face these issues and discover why conformity and control were issues. I learned through this confrontation that my reactiveness could be attributed to a high anxiety state driven by feelings of fear, insecurity, anger, and helplessness. My children and marriage suffered a lot from this high anxiety state because I felt as though I lacked control of what was happening to me in that family system. It was the same lack of control I felt when I lived at home with my father and siblings. It was the same constant questioning of my ability to be productive and able to make contributions. Just thinking about becoming just another face in the crowd frightened me, causing me to either rebel or withdraw inside myself.

I was eventually able to trace this unrealistic expectation and fear to my stay hospitalization as a small child, where I had no control over what, when, or how I played or moved within the ward or my bed. My physical movement was limited by restraints that kept me confined to the bed majority of the time. Oftentimes I had to compete with the other kids to get the nurses' attention. *Is this where my competitive nature was born?* It took three quarters at LIOS before I learned how much the issue of control consumed me unconsciously. It was through the FIRO-B, a quantitative assessment, that I learned of my high need to be in control and not to be controlled. The FIRO-B helps individuals understand their behavior and the behavior of others; measures interpersonal needs in three areas such as inclusion, control, and affection. It also identifies options for increasing job satisfaction and productivity and becoming effective in one-on-one coaching, team-building and leadership development. This assessment taught me that my high need for control, whether conscious or unconscious, lessens my ability to be a competent group member or leader.

The Third Mentor

My third mentor was an African-American woman and my supervisor at the bank. She took me under her wing at the workplace and re-introduced me to the African-American community. My family had already lived in the area for seven years but had previously experienced little contact with the African-American community. This was partly due to the fact that the church my family attended was Catholic and was located on the eastside, whereas the leading churches in the Black community were Baptist and Methodist and located in Seattle. Only years later was the eastside Catholic Church that Blacks attended brought to my attention. Except for my favorite aunts, who were decreased by this time, this thoughtful woman was the first African-American woman to take the time to teach me how to reach out to our community. In doing so, she taught me the value of a positive sense of community. This value was to become a principle driver in my life. The earlier mentors in my life stimulated what was always kept safe within me: my values and emotional temperament. These mentors exemplified courage and compassion that I learned to integrate into my healing process. Through their interventions I adopted new values that transcended self-interest and control, strengthening my ability to seek intimacy and the unconditional love of self and others.

Personal Values and Emotional Well-being

While participating in the Educational Leadership degree program at Seattle University, my cohort was asked to complete a values inventory survey created by Hall (1994). According to Hall (1994, p. 21), "values are the ideals that give significance to our lives, that are reflected through the priorities that we choose, and that we act on consistently and repeatedly." Similar to Hall, I believe that values drive the decisions and behavior of individuals. Hall's survey identified how my personal values, such as caring, listening and supporting others drove my leadership style as a facilitator, collaborator and servant. This inventory also highlighted my need to be intrapersonal and communal when working with employees or in situations that require peer participation. This useful tool also identified my level of intensity as high for my mission and called to the need for interdependent action. Another observation of interest was mentioned under the category world-view, reflecting the fact that I am beginning to see the world with less relativism. This happens when one can start to see concepts such as right and wrong, goodness and badness, and truth and falsehood are not absolute but change from culture to culture and situation to situation. This new insight created a personal mission and a place for me to emerge.

My values' analysis indicated that I had a critical future role in institutional leadership. The results of the values inventory pointed out that I would find it important to discover ways to utilize the plural we instead of the singular I to help institutions become more humane. Through the values inventory, I learned that I had selected 'being self' as being a high value for me. Hall (1990) defined 'being self' as the capacity to own one's truth about self and the world. He thought this value demonstrated an increased awareness of personal strengths and one's limitations, as well as the ability to act independently and cooperatively when appropriate (p.226). This information enabled me to understand what helped me get through so many of my traumatic experiences.

Moustakas (1990, p. 99) would describe this transformation as a symbolic growth experience; when an internal change or revision in how one remembers an experience alters one's frame of reference or worldview. This was the first time I was truly free to put myself first and not others. After I separated for the first time from my husband, I used my time to strengthen myself spiritually, mentally and physically. This included learning how to become intimate with my older children.

Intimacy was one of my growing edges, especially as a parent. My children were eleven and eight at the time and remained in my care after he left. Although they saw their father every other weekend, they were angry and blamed me for their father leaving them behind. I acknowledged their anger and blame, and then went about teaching them both how to survive by helping me budget for food and clothing. It was uncomfortable for me to cuddle or hold my children close. As an older adult, cuddling and hugging has become more natural to me now, than in the past. My issues around intimacy unconsciously kept my husband at a distance when he returned home and for the next nine years we tried to rebuild our marriage. During this same period of time, I sought out ways to advance myself without returning to college. Through my supervisor and mentor at work, I learned of a then newly created program called Leadership Tomorrow. With my mentor's coaching and encouragement, I was eventually nominated by a lifelong female friend for entrance into the program. This nomination became a controversy at the financial institution where I worked because the officers of that organization had not nominated me as their representative. They had submitted the name of an assistant vice president to represent the financial institution. However, the program selection committee chose me, and I joined the fourth class of Leadership Tomorrow.

My entrance into Leadership Tomorrow marked the beginning of my civic involvement. By 1989, one year after graduating, my thirst for knowledge in the civic and public arena had grown and led me to pursue a master's degree in business and public administration at City University. I later changed my focus to applied behavioral science. Little did I know that this decision to return to school would eventually help close a twenty year chapter of my life; three years later my husband and I finally divorced. By this time our daughter was attending college, our son had two more years remaining in high school. This is when I was first becoming conscious of my issues around intimacy and began to reach out physically to my children; but they were angry at me again. It was a bitter pill to swallow when my first attempts at creating closeness were rejected, but this was what I had taught them through my own patterns of behavior.

The Fourth Mentor

After my life changing experiences in Leadership Tomorrow, and my growing thirst for more civic involvement, my next baptism occurred within the Democratic Party. This is when my fourth mentor entered my life in 1988. Before a political party nominates their front runner for President, there are layered elections at the local level. First, a potential nominee has to be elected or appointed as a Precinct Committee Officer (PCO), who is responsible for sharing political materials within an assigned precinct informing citizens about their party candidates and encouraging them to vote. The first level of elections is at the Legislative District Caucus, where an individual prepares and presents a speech before the members of their

Legislative District. Once elected at this level, the PCO's then attend the Congressional District Caucus. This is the last level leading up to the State Convention where members converge statewide to vie for the final available slots. This mentor taught me how to network and leave a memorable mental calling card about myself when doing so. Because of her ingenuity, tenacity, and endurance we stayed up for twenty four hours which led to my election as a Washington State delegate at the 1988 Democratic National Convention in Atlanta. During 24 hours of caucuses held throughout the night, with my mentor's guidance, I managed to capture the attention of the group's leaders. These leaders each had one vote toward determining who the last 14 candidates would be. These last slots were coveted by 2,000 delegates who strove to be elected at the state level. Reaching this level of the election to represent Washington State was considered to be one of the most difficult elections to achieve. Especially with only fourteen slots available to a pool of over 2,000 potential delegates. The next morning, names of newly elected delegates were posted, with my name fourth on the list. My mentor's tenacity and belief in my ability to succeed and my own determination were the winning combination that took me to the 1988 Democratic National Convention in Atlanta.

The Fifth Mentor

During 1993, a highly visible and broadly recognized African American female leader whose husband was Mayor at the time, took several women of color under her wing and prepared us to run for elected office. She selected ten women from the King County area who had either expressed an interest in running for office or demonstrated the potential to do so. It was my strong civic involvement that caught the attention of the Mayor's wife. During the next two years, this mentor coached each of us as well as facilitating introductions to those in the community who could help us when we were ready to run for office. The actual impetus that spurred me to run for office happened in 1994 when I attended a workshop on Undoing Racism sponsored by the City of Bellevue. The workshop facilitator sent a clear message that we needed to do something with what we learned and not just walk out the door and hope that someone else would lead the way. At that time, the fabric of Bellevue was changing, and although it was still predominantly White, significant numbers of people from communities of color and Eastern Europe were moving in everyday. There were editorials about these changes and the city's inadequacies in meeting the needs of these newcomers. I submitted one such editorial and it was published in the Seattle-Post Intelligencer in 2003, eight years after my first run for office. I wrote about the changing communities on the eastside:

Longtime Bellevue resident Doreen Cato, founder of Sisters on the Eastside, a group composed of women of color, said she is curious about the hometowns of conference participants. "I hope it's not just Seattle. That's one reason why I'm going," she said. "So much is changing on the Eastside [and] on the north." Cato's organization joined with another group, Eastside Asian Pacific Islanders, to create the Institute for Community Involvement. "We're still reaching the top layer" of activists, Cato said. "The layer we really want to get to are people who for whatever reason are inactive. We're not even a blip on their screens."

The Sixth Mentor

In 1995, I ran for a position on the city council with the guidance of another mentor who was the only female African American state legislator at the time. She had first entered my life in 1985, when she was operating a nonprofit in the Seattle area. Jack and Jill, Inc. was an African American organization that was searching for a community group to partner with in order to apply for a grant from the national office. We were successful in obtaining the grant for her organization, and in time, after she had successfully been elected as a State Representative for two terms she became my mentor. During my second run for office, she made herself available by phone day and night, whenever I needed to call her for advice or just to vent. One thing she told me stays with me to this day. She said, "You will never be a loser in a race. People will remember you for your courage and seek you out." She was right because even though my attempt for office was unsuccessful, I did win. This became evident in my community after my attempt, when it became impossible for me to go anywhere unnoticed. My highly publicized run for office brought with it a much higher level of visibility. Although this attention was unwanted it did enhance my self-esteem, and led me to form a civic group called Sisters on the Eastside.

I crossed the bridge towards self actualization when I finally made the decision to run for elected office. It took an enormous amount of courage for me to make this choice because of the high visibility, loss of privacy; and becoming vulnerable to the opinions and judgments of strangers. Yet, I strongly desired to bring much of what I had internalized into the world; my knowledge, political acumen along with my motivation to minimize the effects of an oppressive state. Facing the last of these desires was the hardest, knowing this race was in a predominantly affluent White community and also that I represented the first and only Black female candidate among five White males. This was one choice that required prayer and faith in God to build my inner capacity to make good decisions, withstand those who opposed me, step out and show myself within a sometimes hostile community and also accept the consequences of my actions.

The hostility in the residential district was mainly directed toward my platform promoting group homes for youth within the community. Other items on my platform included the plan to create more affordable housing, build a facility to expand capacity for the performing arts and offer a better city-wide transit program. However it was my platform to build group homes for youth that created a furor in local residential areas, especially those with homeowners associations. My political opposition used my ethnicity and liberal beliefs to instill fear throughout the community. I was branded a liberal as though it was a dirty word. My favorite public response at those association meetings became "If caring for the welfare of our children and youth makes me a liberal than brand the letter 'L' on my forehead for the entire world to see, because they are our legacy." Ironically my speeches sometimes elicited standing ovations from the very people who demonized me. During the process of running for office, one shining moment came when I received an unexpected call from a stranger alerting me to a negative hit flyer that had been sent around to all the homes in his neighborhood. This White man had heard me speak at one of the community forums, believed the hit flyer was derogatory and wanted me to know about it. He personally delivered a copy of the flyer into my hands. The words on the flyer began with a question written out in capital letters, "DO WE WANT SOMEONE DIFFERENT FROM US TO BE ON THE CITY COUNCIL?" This message went to the core of my old fears and internally oppressive thoughts. However, fortified by new values and belief systems instilled by my mentors I fought these fears and confronted those who tried to stereotype me. These attempts to stereotype me probably left many in the community with frightful thoughts. However this White stranger, who believed in fairness and equity, personally brought this flyer to my attention. This small action from a stranger was a turning point for me. Experiencing this *key* moment was the largest winning factor that simultaneously validated and made up for the many painful moments I experienced during the race. Even though my run for office was unsuccessful, the race ended up as a winning experience because of the courage, tenacity, and integrity I displayed throughout the election. Williams (2002) best describes my political journey with his statement, "Internal assets such as problem-solving skills, a sense of future, and social competence are reported as affecting how a child overcomes challenging circumstances." My inner courage was cultivated and nurtured by supportive adults who coached and guided me through many of the challenges. The learning I gained from each of my six mentors gave me the necessary materials for building a bridge to leadership. Another factor in my successful emergence as a worthy opponent was the education I received in the Leadership Institute of Seattle graduate program of Applied Behavioral Science.

Williams (2002) and other resilience theorists believe there are factors that protect or sensitize children against the hazards of life's traumatic experiences that can help shape them into adaptive adults. These factors are learned from supportive adults in the community such as teachers, clergy, friends and counselors who play an important role in resiliency development. Especially for children whose families are unable to provide them with an optimally supportive environment. Wangari Matthai is one such person who was protected by those in her environment.

CHAPTER THIRTEEN

WANGARI MAATHAI

We moved from self to others, from my issue to our issues,
from home to communities, from national level to global. Now we
embrace the concepts of a global village, our global neighborhood,
our only one planet and our common home and future.

Wangari Maathai, from her 2004 acceptance speech of the
Petra Kelly Prize

Wangari Maathai, a Kikuyu, was considered to be charismatic, humble, and possessed of an illuminating spirit. Like many Kenyans, Maathai came from a farming family. Maathai's home life was very much like other Kenyans as well. Wangari's parents taught her to respect the soil and its generosity in giving. Her father was considered the head of the house and her mother had very little power and performed traditional 'women's tasks' such as fetching water and gathering firewood. Education for women or girls was not valued or encouraged. Maathai grew up close to her mother, working in the fields, which allowed her to observe and appreciate nature. Because she was the eldest, Wangari and her mother spent much time talking. Wangari considered her mother as the anchor in her life. The direct and indirect messages Wangari received from her parents included observing how her mother and father cared for the land, as though it were a member of the family. This modeling encouraged Wangari's future direction. Wangari (2006, p. 13) once said, "My inspiration partly comes from my childhood experiences and observations of nature in rural Kenya."

Many of Wangari's traumatic childhood experiences came during the uprising of the Mau Mau, also known as the freedom fighters. Wangari was twelve years old at the start of this era. At the time, many of her people had to choose whether they would align themselves with the Mau Mau or the British. During the chaos, Wangari's mother and other siblings were confined in what was called an emergency village or detention camp; her father perceived by his people as a corroborator stayed within his employer's compound. One night, due to a raid on her village, Wangari was required to hide in the forest and protect her younger siblings, one of whom was an infant. It so happened that a leopard passed by them in the darkness and Wangari knew that one sound from the baby would cost them their lives. She knew this because Wangari's mother had planted messages conveying the urgency of protecting the young at all costs. These messages were passed from mother to child with the intent of protecting a child of color in a climate of racial discrimination and violence.

Greene, et al (2002) citing Miller and MacIntosh (1999) state, "In their discussion of racial socialization and identity, they [Miller and MacIntosh] pointed out that parental messages given to Black children, whether direct or indirectly, could prepare them to function in an environment of inequality" (p. 242). Positive messages are something that did occur for Wangari, whose close relationship with her mother encouraged the development of her unique and caring spirit that was of great value within her family. Wangari's family also nurtured her excellent mind by sending her away to receive her early education at a primary school run by Italian nuns. She did very well in school, and also kept her close relationship to nature.

This positive messaging also occurred in my own family and I reflect back on how our father encouraged us to take pride in and educate ourselves about our racial heritage. He required the three oldest children in my family to go to the library and read John Hope Franklin's book on Black history. My sister and I sat and read the book while our brother played nearby. Our father also drilled us on what we learned and would punctuate these lessons with statements such as "You will have to work ten times harder than the Whites if you expect to be successful in this world;" and "It is important that you know where you come from so you don't hang your head in shame but hold it up in pride." Our youngest sister missed out on this training and the library intimidated my brother who had trouble reading at the time. Yet, my brother remembered the oral lessons we received from our father in the kitchen of our home. Our father was trying to sensitize us against discrimination as well as racism and classism. Greene, et al (2002) citing McAdoo (1992) states "In the instance of Black parents, they must prepare their children to function in both a Black and White society" (p. 244). Analysis suggests this is exactly what my father was doing with us. Greene's framework for preparing children against an oppressive environment is not limited to one particular ethnic group; it is applicable to any group of people who have experienced oppression.

What does it mean to be raised in an oppressive society? Wangari, in her early years, was unaware that her existence was oppressed. This was because of the protective factors her parents, extended family, and community provided. Greene, et al (2002) writes, "Oppression is a process in which the dominant group in a society imposes a negative view about a minority group's value or place in the world" (p. 248).

Greene (2002, p. 248) also cites hooks (1984), a feminist thinker, who states, "The oppressor group may be thought of as the center or the seat of political, economic, and social power. The oppressor group also has control of resources and dominates the choice of cultural and linguistic forms used in a social structure." Wangari's faith, protective factors and adaptive skills served her into adulthood. As a mother of three, she was also a political activist, feminist, and environmentalist in Kenya. She was determined to be well educated; eventually she earned her Ph.D. and headed the department of a university in Kenya. In the early 1970s, she founded the Green Belt Movement, fighting for the preservation of forests in Kenya and East Africa. This movement helped to restore indigenous forests while assisting rural women in becoming self-sufficient and spread quickly from Kenya across all of Africa. Until her untimely death in September of 2011, Wangari served as an assistant minister for the environment and as a Member of Parliament.

In the past, Wangari Maathai suffered imprisonment, repression and abuse. But nothing could stop her or compromise her ideals. Beyond the ecology movement, she joined the struggle for democratic and social rights of citizens and has been one of the most famous international ambassadors for African women. These facts, along with her courage, insight, determination, and reality-based persistence contributed to the many reasons why she was awarded the Nobel Peace Prize in 2004.

In 2004, Wangari Maathai also received the international Petra Kelly Prize of the Heinrich Böll Foundation for her unique role in African politics, dedication to the green movement in Africa and her lifetime achievements. After the 1990s, Wangari Maathai became increasingly involved in the struggle for human rights and a peaceful multi-ethnic Kenya. At the time this brought her into frequent conflict with the regime and she was repeatedly arrested. Appointed as Assistant Minister in the Ministry of Environment, a position she held from 2003 until 2005, she became part of the new government of Kenya under President Mwai Kibaki. With this involvement, she became the first Green politician in Africa to enter national government.

Wangari Maathai was a woman of power and courage, who set the pace for other African Women. Learning about her after my third visit to Africa brought me a new awareness of how strong African women are in their homeland. There is an African proverb that speaks to this, "If you want to go quickly, go alone; if you want to go far, go together." Wangari was a scion among her people in Kenya, and other women continue to emulate her work by planting trees whenever possible. Notably, when Cultural Reconnection delegates arrived in Africa we were given small trees to plant and name, in order to replenish the earth.

CHAPTER FOURTEEN

CULTURAL RECONNECTION AND AAKEWO

Just don't give up trying to do what you really want to do. Where there is love and inspiration, I don't think you can go wrong.

Ella Fitzgerald

Some of the most rewarding times in my life have been my five years of volunteering in Kenya and Ethiopia with Cultural Reconnection. Cultural Reconnection is an organized delegation of American women of African ancestry who are on a mission to reacquaint themselves and reconnect with their African ancestry. When I joined together with these women I realized that all the lessons I learned with previous mentors had saved only half a portion of the leader within me; it was Cultural Reconnection that succeeded in helping me connect all the dots in my life. As a member in this group, I have built lasting relationships and learned that joy and spirituality are one.

My first glimpse of Africa came in 2004, when a friend and I traveled to Paris and Spain. It was while we were travelling in the southernmost tip of Spain that we were introduced to Africa. During the time we were in Madrid, I mentioned to the apartment manager our plans to travel near the Rock of Gibraltar on the following day. I told him the story my father had shared with me over and over about our beginnings in the Americas. Our family marked their time in the United States by "the time of Pocahontas which would have placed the first person to arrive in the late 1600's. The apartment manager was so enchanted with some of my family stories that he beseeched me to let him take care of the arrangements for the final leg of our trip. After almost missing our connection, we finally arrived to a town named Algeciras a port in the south of Spain, and the largest city on the Bay of Gibraltar. We caught a bus and traveled 15 miles to a very small town that had strong evidence of Moorish history. After throwing my bags in our room, we quickly ran down the stairs to explore. Before we could get out the door, the hotel manager stopped us and asked, "Did we like our room?" My friend and I looked at each other in bewilderment as to why he seemed so intense. Apparently, we gave him an unsatisfactory answer and he took me by my arm back up the stairs. Our rooms were on the very top of the hotel, giving us our own private balcony with a fantastic view on the left of the Rock of Gibraltar. The rest of the view was overcast and misty. He pointed in straight of me and said, "What do you see in front of you?" I said I could barely see evidence of land across from us. He said, "You are looking at your Motherland, Africa!" I almost collapsed to my knees. I cried tears of joy and felt the elation of disbelief as the breeze from the Strait of Gibraltar covered me. *I shed tears of joy at this memory even now.* I could only think that I was the first person from my family since the 1600's to see Africa again. We later took a ferry over to see Tangier, Morocco; even though it was Northern Africa, it was nevertheless the continent of my people.

Cultural Reconnection

This experience led me to Cultural Reconnection. After returning from my trip to Europe and Africa, I was inspired and ready to return to Africa. It was then that I learned about and met a notable leader named Marcia Tate Arunga. Arunga is an African American woman, author, and professor, who married a Kenyan and moved to Kisumu, Kenya for 11 years. While living in Kenya she had four children. Later, upon returning to the United States she cofounded Cultural Reconnection with her sister-in-law Phelgona Arunga. After returning to the United States, I sought out this group that traveled on trips to Africa since the year 2000.

Cultural Reconnection is an organized delegation of women of African ancestry who are on a mission to be re-acquainted with and reconnect with our African ancestry. Each year an organized delegation of women participate in a planned itinerary in Kenya to facilitate their interests and reconnection through relationships with Kenyan women and their families. We find the ways we can connect through common culture. We are also referred to as African American Kenyan Women Interconnect (AAKEWO) working collectively in joint ventures that contribute to a better future for children and their caregivers. We focus on the needs of orphans and vulnerable children living with trauma. Through these joint ventures, sanitary and available water, education and the improvement of health and well being of children and caregivers are increased.

This experience was an inspiration to replicate the principles of Cultural Reconnection in Ethiopia, another African country. I did this with the blessings of the Cultural Reconnection vision and planning team who made it possible to represent the spirit of their work in a very remote section of south-central Ethiopia, called Goba, a village surrounded by mountains and bordered by Somalia and the Northern part of Kenya. In the small Oromo village called Meliyu I was accompanied by two friends who were American Ethiopians who acted as interpreters. Together, we introduced the women of that village to the guiding principles of Cultural Reconnection. These same village women later organized themselves and in two years established a preschool that they named after me.

According to Tate-Arunga (2002, p. 59) Cultural Reconnection is influenced by these guiding principles: collective action, being culturally respectful of rites and practices, practicing shared dialogue and gender specificity. The first principle, *collective action*, supports our efforts to connect, lead, and learn with others. This principle has encouraged 74 African American women, lead by Marcia Tate Arunga, to reach out to hundreds of Kenyan and Ethiopian women. This principle has also taught me how to enhance my interpersonal and communication skills, strengthen and form more significant relationships.

The second principle is about being *culturally respectful of rites and practices,* such as pouring water onto a plant or the ground as a way of inviting past ancestors into the room, and then later releasing them through the same process. Informing and encouraging women who want to go to Africa to embrace and reconnect with African cultural commonalities. These commonalities are rooted in the traditions of our ancestors and often connected to what our parents handed down to us from their African roots. This knowledge is spiritually gratifying on a personal level. During our time in Kenya, and upon our return to the United States, the African American community participated in dialogues with different communities and each other. This taught me how to share our individual experiences, connections, and discoveries

151

with people different from me, yet the same as me. This sharing was a demonstration of the third principle *shared dialogue* that supported our transformation. Sharing took place in mixed gender groupings and with the recognition that males and females view the world and culture in ways that distinguish them separately. There is a very different energy found in and expressed by both genders. The commonality found between women is supported by the last principle of Cultural Reconnection practices, *Gender Specificity*. This principle has shaped not only my ability to connect with my African counterparts, but aided me in moving beyond the negative experiences of slavery and colonialism. These negative experiences, generated in most American communities including my own, include the implanted prejudicial societal perceptions, beliefs and values about Africa and Africans that lead people to portray us as primitive or call us names. Importantly, the principles, mentors and protective skills that Cultural Reconnection offered have provided additional ingredients in my leadership development.

Today, I am the Executive Director of a K-6th free private elementary school and social service agency called First Place. First Place is highly unique in structure, and many have classified what we do as cutting edge. We offer supportive services and housing for families in crisis in addition to culturally competent academic education. Our organization offers diagnostic assessments, counseling, individual mentoring and tutoring, limited onsite healthcare, and community referrals for traumatized families and children. I am blessed with numerous affiliations in the community and have received many awards for my civic engagements and volunteerism; yet it was my childhood upbringing coupled with the people who entered my life by way of their interventions that laid the bricks on my path to leadership.

CHAPTER FIFTEEN

RESEARCH METHODOLOGY

The fact that the adult American Negro female emerges as a formidable character is often met with amazement, distaste and even belligerence. It is seldom accepted as an inevitable outcome of the struggle won by survivors, and deserves respect if not enthusiastic acceptance.

Maya Angelou, I Know Why the Caged Bird Sings, 1969

According to Moustakas (1990, p. 54), "Research is a demanding and lengthy process; and once one enters into the quest for knowledge and understanding, once one begins the passionate search for the illumination of a puzzlement, the intensity, wonder, intrigue, and engagement carry one along through ever growing levels of meaning and excitement." Accordingly, it was exhilarating to find theories, experiences and case studies that corroborated with and validated my research. This was accomplished using databases such as ERIC, The Sociology of Education, The Education Book Review, phenomenology focused websites; published theories and stories on traumatized children who became leaders and social justice articles. Recognizing there are large amounts of quantitative and qualitative information existing on trauma and resiliency, my work centers on the connection between

153

trauma and leadership. This connection forms the bridge that helps to identify the manifesting characteristics of a leader who experienced a traumatic childhood.

The qualitative research methodology used to write *Saving the Leader Within* was taken from Moustakas 's (1990) *Heuristic Research: Design, Methodology & Applications.* Qualitative research requires inquiry and exploration of issues, along with understanding phenomena. In heuristic research, the researcher must have had a direct, personal encounter with the phenomenon being investigated and has endured the experience in a vital and intense way. The heuristic methodology demands the total presence, honesty, maturity, and integrity of a researcher who strongly desires to understand the question. It is essential that the researcher be fully engulfed in the demands of the process. He or she must be willing to commit endless hours of sustained immersion and focused concentration on one or two central questions, and to risk opening old wounds and passionate concerns. This journey took me through a cathartic transformation. There were days, even weeks where it was difficult to come out of the mental hole where I had placed myself and function on a cognitive level. Heuristic research requires the researcher to pursue the 'why' of a subject. This methodology contains five phases: initial engagement, immersion, illumination, explication and creative synthesis to answer the 'why'. According to Moustakas (1990, p. 43), there are four widely accepted approaches to planning and conducting a phenomenological investigation (Gall et al, 2003, p. 481-482):

First, the researcher must identify a topic of personal and social significance. This approach speaks to engaging the researcher intellectually and emotionally. The personal connection to the topic encourages the researcher to collect data on his or her own experience of the phenomena. Second, the researcher must select appropriate participants. Husserl (as cited by Gall, et al (2003, p. 482) believed, that through a process of empathy a researcher can begin to understand another person's experience as it correlates to his or her own. My immediate family consisting of my widowed father and two sisters were participants in this research. Third, the researcher must interview each participant. While conducting this phenomenological research, the researcher conducts a long interview with each participant in order to obtain a comprehensive description of his or her experience. This is designed to lead to comprehension of the phenomena being studied. Fourth, the researcher must analyze the interview data. Data analysis in phenomenological research generally follows the procedures of case study analysis. The interview data for each case is broken into segments; the researcher looks for meaning units and themes in the segments; the meaning units and themes are compared across cases; and finally, the case findings are synthesized and validated by checking with the participants. Merriam (1998, p.158) cautions that, "suspension of judgment is critical in a phenomenological investigation and requires the setting aside of the researcher's personal viewpoint in order to see the experience for itself."

The heuristic methodology requires the substantial use of inquiry and self-discovery that is the principal approach to conducting this study. This research is conducted in five phases; by using the theoretical framework of initial engagement, immersion, incubation, illumination, explication, and creative synthesis this study took on a life of its own.

Initial Engagement

The catalyst for this research emerged out of a previous qualitative study in which an interview conducted with my youngest sister became the pivotal reason for writing *Saving the Leader Within*. This interaction was the initial engagement for my research study and was presented at Seattle University 2005 Leadership Conference on Poverty and Education (Cato, 2004). This phase requires approaching participants with questions that inquire:

- What does this person know about the experience being studied?
- What qualities or dimensions of the experience stand out for the person?
- What events, situations, and people are connected with the experience?
- What feelings and thoughts are generated by the experience?
- What bodily states or shifts in bodily presence occur in the experience?
- What time/space factors affect the awareness and meaning of the experience?
- Has the person shared all of the significant ingredients of the experience?

This approach led to the emergence of forgotten memories for both the researcher and the participants. These revelations also led me to rethink my own journey, in addition to how my father and others' messages had affected our lives. Moustakas (1990, p. 47) states, "Dialogue is the preferred approach, in that it aims toward encouraging expression, elucidation, and disclosure of the experience being investigated." Through dialogue my sister and I both learned that my sister perceived messages from our father as weapons whose intentions were responsible for her life path. This innocent, informal conversation led to other intense memories that were filled with compelling social and personal implications (Moustakas, 1990, p. 27). My family's responses in the face-to-face interviews were revealing. The process of seeking clarity led each of us to view one another differently. To paraphrase Defrain (1999), no matter how dysfunctional a family may be, they are also likely to have some strength that can become the foundation for healthy new directions; and that a crisis in life can be a catalyst for positive growth. In essence, there is always reason for hope, no matter how desolate one's life may appear.

Immersion

This phase is described by Moustakas (1990. p.28) who notes, "Once the question is discovered and its terms defined and clarified the researcher lives the question in waking, sleeping, and even dream states." The immersion process leads the researcher to comprehend the meaning of the critical question: how is it possible that some children who experience traumatic episodes transcend to become leaders? An immersion inquiry is one's story in its purest form, told without interruptions or clarifications. Moustakas (1990, p. 28) believes a researcher must come to intimate terms with the question in order to live and grow in the understanding that is gained.

By probing my unconscious during the immersion phase and inquiring, "How is it possible that some children who experience traumatic episodes transcend to become leaders?" I brought formerly repressed memories to the surface. The work of this phase led me to deeply explore the relationship between cultural context, language and its impact on behavior. According to Hayakawa & Hayakawa (1990, p.65):

With words, therefore, we influence and to an enormous extent control future events. It is for this reason that writers write; preachers preach; employers, parents and teachers scold; propagandists send out news releases; politicians give speeches. All of them for various reasons are trying to influence our conduct, sometimes for our own good, sometimes for their selves.

This statement validates the pursuit of this research; to show the connection between language and messaging and how they play a vital role in transcending a traumatized childhood. I experienced the immersion phase as a deepening process through a metacognitive approach to thinking. Jennifer Livingston (1997) in her paper "Metacognition: An Overview" defines metacognition as "thinking about thinking." This technique of thinking about my thoughts allowed me to access memories that were formerly hidden within my unconscious mind as a form of self-protection. As Livingston (1997) believes, thinking about one's thoughts and expressing them in writing can lead an individual deeper into critical thinking. Chapter one illustrates the effects of this technique, as I share one such memory that emerged during an experiential exercise while attending LIOS Graduate College, a center for progressive leadership education. Chapter one also presents the three phases of immersion, incubation, and illumination that each examine both conscious and unconscious memories.

Incubation

The incubation phase helped me to take a step back and adopt a third person perspective. Moustakas (1990, p. 28) states, "Incubation is the process in which the researcher retreats from intense, concentrated focus on the question." This phase brings revelations into awareness, such as how my relationship with my father changed through a heartfelt discussion about the past. This phase of the process gave me two additional gifts:

(a) It brought authenticity to my writing and allowed me to incorporate this authenticity into the literature.
(b) It allowed personal internal thoughts that were based on intuition to be clarified and validated (Moustakas 1990).

This phase assisted me in recognizing the distortions inherent in my past memories and revealed hidden meanings that had formerly been unconsciously locked away. Moustakas (1990) believes this period marks a time when participants are in a more receptive state of mind and insight or adjustments may occur. This part of the process allowed me to walk through the landscape of my memories pain free. I gained insight from looking back through a magnifying glass on past relationships, perceived and real abuses, and issues of class, institutional racism, and prejudice. The incubation phase required thoughtful planning about how best to bring my family's case history into fruition.

Illumination

The third phase of this research is the illumination phase. This phase presents itself through the themes, qualities, and patterns of the emerging phenomenon. The researcher and the interviewees co-create a valid depiction of the experience being investigated, and engages in discovering the meaning of the experience through a personal and a disciplinary lens. In this way, formerly misunderstood realities are exposed and the truth of the experience stands revealed. According to Moustakas (1990, p. 30), this phase heralds nuances in meaning and the "discovery of something that has been present for some time yet beyond immediate awareness."

Illumination is a spiritual or intellectual enlightenment which has a direct parallel to one of the protective factors, emotional development and spirituality. According to Webster's dictionary, spirituality relates to or affects the human spirit or soul as opposed to material or physical things. There were many moments during this research process that brought me to tears, caused subtle internal shifts and nurtured my soul. Spirituality can difficult to explain or describe, especially when it is put into the realm of church membership or specific religious beliefs. Moustakas (1990) believes that in the illumination phase, an awakening occurs to bring new insight to elements of an experience that participants were unable to recall earlier. This is what Moustakas (1990, p. 30) refers to as inferred knowledge and intuitive dimensions; a phase when an illuminating experience sheds light on either misunderstood or distorted realities. The experience of illumination is often unanticipated. What is essential is an open mind that will allow access to essential components of a memory that can help reveal the truth of an experience. This particular phase occurred when I captured a metacognitive thought and then integrating it into my writing. For example, in a flash of illumination, I realized my father left me at the hospital because he was trying to save my life when I had formerly remembered this experience only as pure abandonment. I realized he had saved my life while writing about the experience and at the same time thinking about what I had written. These metacognitive thoughts were the key to accessing my unconscious memories.

Explication

The third phase is the explication method. Moustakas (1990, p.31) explains the purpose of this phase, "is to fully examine what awakened in consciousness, in order to understand its various layers of meaning." This phase helps explain the why of traumatic experiences and assists in the reclamation of joy, innocence, hope, and spiritual renewal. It is through explication that the researcher connects understanding to meaning by honing the information down into a narrative form; using responses from verbatim conversations during interviews, excerpts from written case studies or other documents that collaborate with the research.

The explication phase helped me to capture the essence of the impact of childhood trauma on leadership. Gardner (1995, p. 33) believed "Leaders often exhibit the wounds from their early losses and have tenacity, even ruthlessness that may prove difficult for others to comprehend."

Gardner also cites Winston Churchhill's comments taken from his father, John Churchhill's biography:

Famous men are usually the product of an unhappy childhood. The stern compression of circumstances, the twinge of adversity, the spur of slights and taunts in early years are needed to evoke that ruthless fixity of purpose and tenacious mother-wit without which great actions are seldom accomplished.

Gardner (1990) states "Leaders come in many forms, with many styles and diverse qualities. There are quiet leaders, and leaders one can hear in the next country; some find their strength in eloquence, some in judgment, and some in courage" (p.5). In my life, it was my paternal grandmother who was a model of courage and hope, qualities she instilled in me during the two years we lived together while I was attending college.

The purpose of the explication phase is to bring clarity to the immersion, incubation and illumination phases. The explication process unveils the unspoken knowledge gained from the themes, thoughts, qualities and elements of the traumatic experiences. Moustakas (1990, p. 31) states this "phase is to fully examine what has awakened in consciousness, in order to understand its various layers of meaning." The explication phase captured the essence of the impact of childhood trauma on leadership.

Creative Synthesis

The final phase of the heuristic research process happens after the researcher is thoroughly familiar with his or her data, obtained from their co-investigators, along with the qualities, themes and the explication of meanings. Moustakas (1990, p. 31) states the "Creative synthesis can only be achieved through tacit and intuitive powers." The final phase emerges from the participants' experiences and the researcher's personal knowledge of the phenomena, and the creative synthesis takes shape as an artistic representation of the findings. Creative synthesis could take the shape of an art form created by the researcher or might be discovered in the form of a story, music, poem, painting, sculpture or any other innovative form which supports the researcher's knowledge and passion of the experience. After experiencing several deeply impactful revelations I illustrated creative synthesis through writing a poem:

Do I dare take a chance and poke my head outside?

Do I dare take a chance and let my heart accept that ride?

Is it my fault if my soul goes along too? Do I dare take a chance?

Yes I will take the chance to let all of me outside and ride.

Doreen Cato (2007)

During this phase, I found solace in using purposeful poems, quotes and inscriptions to inspire as well as frame my thoughts. The information I had gathered during the immersion, incubation, illumination, and explication phases uniquely positioned me to use imagination and insight to express an artistic version of the themes and critical meanings of the phenomena. As the researcher, the explication phase allowed me to reveal a human experience through language. This phase elevated dialogue into artistic expression, a medium that mirrors the soul and spirituality of humanity.

Case Study Methodology and Application

I utilized two approaches during this research; the primary method was heuristic applications followed by case study methodology. The case study was conducted with the help of members from my immediate family and also through the use of other case studies, personal journals, videos, observations, and scholarly research documents on trauma, resiliency, cultural context, language, and social injustice. As the researcher, my family provided ready access for examining our family's values and the traumatic experiences we endured with an insiders' perspective. This research entailed asking my family members informal questions during conversation modeled on those found in *The Black*

Extended Family. The use of open-ended questions is considered a qualitative approach.

According to Merriam (1998, p. 7), the researcher for a case study is the primary instrument for data collection and analysis, as compared to inanimate devices that are also used for gathering information, such as inventories, computers, recorders, and questionnaires. Using the case study approach requires fieldwork to observe behavior. In order to become intimate with the phenomenon being observed this was a necessary approach. Our experience of the appearance of things, or how we experience them, is the study of phenomena or phenomenology. Merriam (1998, p. 12-20) also states that a case study is a qualitative research method that can "capture intensive descriptions and analyses of a single unit or bounded system." Additionally Merriam states, "A case study might also build a substantive theory." One example is *The Black Extended Family* by Martin and Martin (1978), an ethnographic case study on African-American family values.

Phenomenology

The concept of phenomenology originates in a philosophical movement founded by Edmund Husserl (Gall, Gall and Borg, 2003). Husserl cited by Gall, et al, believed that the starting point for knowledge began with the individual's experience with various sensations, perceptions, and ideals that appear in his or her consciousness" (p. 481). The Stanford Encyclopedia of Philosophy (2003, p.1) states that phenomenological studies are a conscious experience as experienced from the subjective or first person point of view. These experiences are the phenomena. Many of these phenomena in *Saving the Leader Within* were caused by various types of experiences and taken from my perceptions, thoughts, and memories, including my imagination, emotions, desires, bodily awareness, actions, and language (Merriam & Simpson, 2000; Gall, et al, 1999). As Moustakas (1990, p. 97-98) explains, "the task of imaginative variation is to seek possible meanings through the utilization of imagination, varying the frames of reference, employing polarities and reversals, and approaching the phenomenon from divergent perspectives, different positions, roles, or functions." A phenomena or phenomenon, for the purposes of this research study means whatever one observes or perceives and seeks to explain. It may be a reality or perceived to be. Phenomenology uses experience and interpretation to focus on the structural essence of the phenomenon, for example, the essence of being traumatized, or experiencing loneliness, or hope (Merriam 1998; Patton 1990). Another researcher in the arena of phenomenology is Spiegelberg (1965, p. 659) who is considered one of the main architects of phenomenological research methods. He states that "a researcher must first have an 'intuitive grasp' of the phenomenon." Similarly, Merriam (1998, p.16) claims that "a researcher must follow up by investigating several instances or examples of the phenomenon to gain a sense of its general essences."

The Nature of Trauma

Saving the Leader Within focuses primarily on the impact of childhood trauma on leadership. Levine and Fredrick (1997, p. 19) state, "Most of us have experienced some form of trauma from natural disasters, exposure to violence, surgery, medical or dental procedures, difficult pregnancies and births." They also believe that the onset of triggered symptoms from traumatic events causes a freezing state. This freezing state is created at the time of the traumatic event causing the fearful energy to become trapped.

Levine, et al (1997) also notes, "Trauma is often times regarded by psychologists and psychiatrists as being caused by a stressful occurrence outside the range of usual human experience" (p. 24). Leary (2005, p. 14) defines it as an injury caused by an outside, usually violent, force, event, or experience. An experience that is physical, emotional, psychological, or spiritual. She goes on to describe distortions in attitudes can cause:

> If a trauma is severe enough, it can distort our attitudes and beliefs such distortions often result in dysfunctional behaviors, this can in turn produce unwanted consequences. If one traumatic experience can result in distorted attitudes, dysfunctional behaviors and unwanted consequences, this pattern is magnified exponentially when a person repeatedly experiences severe trauma, and it is much worse when the traumas are caused by human beings.

Many ethnic groups have suffered traumatic social injustices that would be distressing to any group. Many of these traumas are passed on as intergenerational traumas. Intergenerational traumas are perpetuated through emotionally and psychologically abusive behaviors. Groups including the Jews, Croatians, Irish, Polish, Africans, American Indians, Spanish, Asians, Pacific Islanders and African-Americans along with many others have experienced horrific traumas. In spite of these traumatic histories each of these groups has produced outstanding leaders throughout history. Leary (2005, p. 15) points out that "the slave experience was one of continual, violent attacks on body, mind, and spirit. Yet many of the African-Americans managed the preservation of family, retained a sense of culture, maintained their humanity, as well as safeguarded their spiritual integrity in an all-too-often inhumane environment."

Schauer, Neuner, and Elbert (2005, p. 5), define psychological trauma as "the experience and psychological impact of events that are life-threatening or include a danger of injury so severe that the person is horrified, feels helpless, and experiences a psycho physiological alarm response during and shortly following the experience"

Psychological trauma is the unique individual experience of an event or enduring conditions, in which "the individual's ability to integrate his or her emotional experience is overwhelmed or the individual experiences (subjectively) a life threatening situation, bodily integrity, or sanity as identified by Pearlman & Saakvitne (1995); Ungar (2004); Brooks & Goldstein (2004); Leary (2005); Harris (1998); and James (1989). The traumatic event commonly includes abuse of power, betrayal of trust, entrapment, helplessness, pain, confusion, and/or loss. There is also intergenerational trauma. An example of intergenerational trauma is passing on traumatic experiences that caused injury physically, emotionally, psychologically, and or spiritually into the next generations. This is often done through oral history by parents or others who have a relationship to the traumatic events; for example the events associated with the holocaust, slavery, genocide, Wounded Knee, detention camps or internment. These include all traumatic experiences that occurred in the past and which are passed down, whether consciously or unconsciously, to the next generation (Leary, 2005).

Intergenerational trauma was described by Leary (2005) as when a slave mother, in an attempt to protect her children in an oppressive and dangerous environment, will choose to play down their attributes. Many African-American parents continue this form of now unnecessary protection. This old protective model can cause children who hear these criticisms and lack an understanding of the historical reasons behind this behavior to feel humiliated and experience emotional injury.

In many cases, culture or cultural context was a strong influence behind many of the traumatic experiences of all those depicted in this research. Cultural context is defined by our upbringing and includes one's belief systems, values, norms and religious background. According to Banks and Banks (2004), cultural context refers to thoughts, opinions and feelings that result from experiences. It is all around us, and is personal, familial, communal, institutional, societal, and global in its scope. Culture influences our thoughts, ideas, behavior patterns, customs, values, skills, language, socioeconomics, arts, faith or religion. Recognizing how each of us is influenced by more than one culture, it is not surprising how cultural complexities play out in families, communities, and workplaces.

Resiliency

Jordan (Brooks & Goldstein, 2003) in her article *Relational Resilience in Girls* defines resiliency "as the ability to bounce back from adversity, to manage stress effectively, and to withstand physical or psychological pressures without showing major debilitation or dysfunction" (p. 79).

Ann Masten (1997), a pioneer in the study of resiliency, cited by Ungar (2005, p. 5) defines it as a class of phenomena characterized by good outcomes in spite of serious threats to adaptation or development. Resiliency is also the ability to seek out flexible factors that will allow one to adapt to adversity, by using an innate ability to self-right oneself to have a successful life. Masten (1997) in her article *Resilience in Children At-Risk* asks, "How do children and adolescents 'make it' when their development is threatened by poverty, neglect, maltreatment, war, parents disabled by physical or mental illness, or natural disasters?" She has learned that outcomes generally worsen as risk factors pile up in children's lives, and concurrently, resilience becomes less common (Masten & Wright, 1997; Garmezy & Masten, 1995; and Egeland, Carlson, & Sroufe, 1993). At catastrophic levels of trauma, no child is expected to be resilient until a safe and more normative environment for development is restored. In cases of massive trauma due to war or chronic child abuse, resilience refers to good recovery after trauma has ended. It is also possible for a child to be resilient and still suffer from residual effects of trauma. In her article *Resilience in Children At-Risk* Masten (1997, p. 2) states, "Resilience does not mean 'invulnerable' or 'unscathed!'" Masten goes on to state: "The possibility that resilient individuals may not escape adversity unscathed has been examined in a study of competent inner city adolescents by Luthar (1991)." She finds that most competent youth, struggling daily with the burdens of poverty and often racism, showed signs of internal distress. This suggests that youth pay a toll in the struggle to overcome adversity, exacted from either the level of adversity itself or the strain of rising above it. Studies of Cambodian youth who survived the holocaust in their country to immigrate to Minnesota also suggest there may be long term consequences of severe adversity. Hubbard et al (1995, p.3) points out, "Years after their war experiences many of these youth still have symptoms of trauma and emotional disturbance, including nightmares, difficulty concentrating, horrifying memories, jumpiness, or times of great sadness. At the same time, these young survivors are getting on with their lives, going to college, making friends, and building constructive lives as they adapt to life in Minnesota. Their lives are a testimony to the astonishing human capacity for resilience."

According to Jordan (Brooks et al, 2003), "resilience is described as: (1) good outcomes in high-risk children; (2) sustained competence in children under stress; and (3) recovery from trauma." However, the subject of recovery from trauma needs to be explored more thoroughly because my research demonstrates there can be perceived recovery from traumatizing events, yet future conditions or similar nonthreatening occurrences are known to trigger emotional responses originating in past traumas. These emotional reactions are often expressions of the same feelings and physical responses that were experienced during the original traumatic event. This phenomenon can occur throughout one's life, and recovery from these experiences as Hartling, 2003; Masten, Best, & Garmezy, 1990). Masten (1997) cited by Benson, Galbraith, & Espenland (1995, p. 79) are "resources in a child's life that may effectively counterbalance high risk." This counterbalance of positive resources is often carried into adulthood.

The Search Institute describes these resources in terms of asset-building. Two cities in Washington State: Seattle and Bellevue participated in a national survey that helped to identify the 40 developmental assets. These developmental assets are necessary to create good outcomes for high-risk children and youth. One developmental asset is a caring adult who listens, Ungar (1963, p. 17) asked, "Who is going to listen to children tell it like it is when their voices are largely silenced? We pay inadequate attention to the context in which research and clinical practice takes place, failing to recognize that what we know is skewed by how we go about the business of knowing."

How does listening contribute or not contribute to resiliency? It is important to let children and youth know that they are heard. It is even more important when they are seeking advice or help from an abuser. Brooks and Goldstein (2003, p. 117) state, "We must also learn to validate what others are saying and confirm that they have been heard. It is important to remember that validation does not imply that we agree with the views of other people, but simply acknowledge and respect their perspective." Listening does contribute to resiliency. A child who experiences a traumatic episode needs to know that the community values them, which is identified as one of the 40 developmental assets. A young person then perceives that adults in the community do care for them (Casey, 2005; Brooks and Goldstein, 2003).

Developmental assets are resiliency factors as defined in Search Institute's (1997) 40 developmental assets. They can also be defined as building blocks for healthy development which help young people grow up to be healthy, caring, and responsible. The 40 Developmental assets are a framework for providing young people with positive experiences discovered within themselves as well as within their environment. The assets identify the roles that families, schools, congregations, neighborhoods, and youth organizations can play in promoting healthy development. Internal assets are identified as those characteristics and behaviors that reflect positive internal growth and development (Casey, 2001).

An important ingredient for resiliency, in addition to the 40 developmental assets, is accepting oneself and others. Brooks and Goldstein (2003, p. 137) state "our feelings and thoughts direct our behavior and the ways we cope. If we do not take the time, to identify and reflect on our emotions and beliefs we are vulnerable, not only to acting impulsively but to perpetuating the negative cycles existing in our lives."

This statement is true. It was only after conquering my fears and learning to embrace my feelings that I began to heal. Many traumatized youth and adults adhere to self-defeating internalized scripts. They oftentimes project their rage, disappointments, and frustrations outward at others. Brooks and Goldstein (2003, p. 117) note how they have "observed many people wearing blinders when it comes to recognizing their emotions, understanding what triggers these emotions, and sensing how they are perceived by others." In the past these blinders served as conscious or unconscious coping mechanisms in a hostile environment, whether perceived or real. One thing is certain most survivors who eventually forgive, find it difficult to forget.

CHAPTER SIXTEEN

REFLECTIONS

Do I dare take a chance and poke my head outside?
Do I dare take a chance and let my heart accept that ride?
Is it my fault if my soul goes along too? Do I dare take a chance?
Yes I will take the chance to let all of me outside and ride.

Doreen Harden-Cato (2007)

I experienced cathartic learning as I delved into my own and others' experiences, especially in dialogue with members of my family. As James Baldwin, author of *The Fire Next Time*, once wrote, "Know whence you came. If you know whence you came, there is really no limit to where you can go." In keeping with these words, my research revealed that childhood trauma taught me to adapt, develop self-efficacy, grow emotionally, recognize my spiritual connection and strive for self-actualization. These same protective factors allowed Sojourner Truth, Eleanor Roosevelt, Dr. Martin Luther King Jr., and Wangari Maathai to find the pathway to leadership, and promoted my capacity to lead.

Researching and writing this book has required that I revisit disturbing and painful memories from childhood, as well as process repressed memories that emerged unbidden during the immersion phase of the heuristic research process. I experienced skepticism and fear when it came to pursuing this particular research methodology and was unprepared for the emotional journey these research methods would require. Looking back at each phase of this process is interesting; very little pain or fear remains. The immersion phase was the hardest. I experienced strong resistance to letting go and allowing myself to feel the old emotions and physical discomforts that came along with this process. Overriding this discomfort took time. Utilizing my own family for the case study gave me ready and intimate access to traumas that occurred during my childhood and all the way through my young adulthood.

I want to share what occurred for me, both emotionally and mentally, during each of the following phases: initial engagement, immersion, incubation, illumination, explication, and creative synthesis and how this approach helped to flush out similarities between my traumatic experiences and what may have manifested for the historical and notable leaders identified for *Saving the Leader Within.*

Initial Engagement

This first step was initially laid out for me when I interviewed my youngest sister for a different research paper entitled, "Poverty and Education." Her response to the interview questions were moving and caused me to ask the first question, "Why did you choose not to go to college?" Her response to that question lingered with me for a year and led me to formulate the eventual research question for *Saving the Leader Within*, "how is it possible that some children who experience traumatic episodes transcend to become leaders?" I wanted to discover why all four of us ended up so differently and yet experienced so many of the same things. We witnessed each others' pain, humiliations, joys, and celebratory moments. Yet it seemed our emotional and mental scars still prevented us from experiencing fully all the happier moments in our lives. I learned this from speaking with my two sisters. My brother was more difficult for me to approach because his behavior sometimes reminded me of my father's darker side, and triggered old and fearful responses. It was more comfortable for me to write about him from my memories than from current observations. I still feared the father of my childhood and my perception of my brother was the personification of this ghost from my past. Even though I am the oldest, it was hard for me to shake those old images and messages that came to mind when thinking of my brother.

Yet, I was able to approach my father while he was still alive in order to validate some of my old memories. My only explanation for this is that my father had grown much older and was mellow at age eighty-three, whereas my brother was the spitting image of the younger version of my father, as I remembered him.

Immersion

The second phase was immersion which reached memories I was shocked to learn existed. This particular phase took me two years to get through. During that time I lost my sibling who was fourteen months younger than me from a massive heart attack. I was devastated by her death and felt the old pain of betrayal. This sister was the one who attempted suicide at eleven and again at eighteen. I know she refused to go to the doctor even though my father and I both told her to go. In dying, I believe she finally got her wish. *I just recognized this as a child's response of blaming myself for not being more insistent that she see the doctor.* Rationally, what could I do to help her from 3000 miles away, but my father's old message of being the oldest with the responsibility to protect those younger than me is ever present. This behavior shows up even today in my role as executive director, when I consciously and unconsciously interpret my responsibility for the staff as a big sister who seeks to protect them from a hostile environment, whether perceived or real.

During the immersion period, I experienced a very painful moment when writing about the uncaring community that surrounded me during my childhood. It happened during a business trip to Washington D.C. and late at night. Letting myself totally submerge in that painful time, I found myself crying uncontrollably and rocking back and forth with my arms wrapped tightly around me. My feelings were about being totally abandoned by those who could have saved us, but instead turned their eyes and ears away from our plight. I realized this thought while submerging deeper to seek the answer to the research question. Later in the course of writing there were other similar incidents that occurred related to the impact of childhood trauma on leadership. And although, there were many solemn memories, there were also many memories that provided me with great feelings of elation such as the freedom march in Detroit, family trips, and certain relatives who were there for us when possible.

Incubation

One family trip not shared earlier in the book that just came to me unbidden; it is one of those stories that bring feelings of excitement mixed with uncertainty. At the time, my father wanted us to see the locks in Sault Saint Marie, Ontario Canada by way of Northern Michigan.

We as children were unaware of the Jim Crow rules that caused my father to be so wary on the trip. *I remember in my mind's eye seeing him bite his bottom lip as he drove.* Being the oldest, it was my job to be navigator. It was a privilege I looked forward to taking on whenever we traveled. Whenever we took those long trips my father always packed a large picnic basket filled with sandwiches, potato chips, fruit, napkins, and utensils; along with plenty of his favorite lemonade, and packages of Kool-Aide, if we ran out of the lemonade. He also brought a large jar for us to pee in during the ride in the car. *I often wondered why we couldn't just pull over and go in the bushes.* I recognize as an adult that these were precautionary measures taken to preserve our safety from being harassed and to prevent the possibility of my father being arrested. He took care of all of these details of preparation just because he wanted us to see how the large ships that came through the locks on Lake Superior to the Atlantic Ocean. We were unaware that Blacks were unable to find accommodations or food along the way to Sault Saint Marie. My father was only allowed to buy gas. It was a long trip to Canada, which my father had to drive in two days. One day to get us there and the other to get us back. He pulled off the road on the return trip so that all of us could sleep. As children, we thought this was all just a part of our exciting trip. We did not know that our father was only trying to keep us safe and protect us from knowledge of Jim Crow. This is basically what the incubation phase did for me and is still doing, making me see my memories differently and guiding me to illumination.

Illumination

It was during this phase that I began to gain insight into why certain memories were so explosive for me. Really stepping back and looking at them through adult eyes made me see a clearer picture. It was literally like the lights were turned up and I could examine all those bad things in the shadows that were not always what my mind had come to believe. I came to the realization that many pieces of past incidents had broader explanations than what I could ascertain as a child. This knowledge does not diminish in any way the sexual, emotional, and physical abuse we endured, but makes me see my father's role in a different light. His task as a single parent trying to raise four children, three of them girls, was a hard road to walk. He did this without a book or map on how to be a single parent raising four children and work two jobs at the same time. As children, we had no knowledge of what it took for our father to get up go to work every day only to return in the evening to four small children. We were his Friday night date. I remember one Friday night when all of us were suppose to be asleep, hearing him cry deep from his belly, while sitting on the steps that led to the bedroom I shared with my sisters. I wanted to go to him, but was afraid to as he was crying softly so as not to wake us. Even then I understood he was deeply hurt, lonely, and ashamed to show his grief and so tried to do it without us knowing. This was a moment of illumination for me. As an adult, the explanations for many of those moments are more understandable.

Explication

This phase took place in third person and for this reason was easier than the immersion, incubation, and illumination phases for me to work through. The three previous phases continually pulled me back into stronger emotions that were difficult to set aside without withdrawing entirely from the writing process for weeks. The explication phase made me look at the 'why' of those past episodes from a clinical perspective. The explanations for many of those memories made me realize what characteristics manifested during those experiences. Looking at the courage it required as children to figure out how to fight back, even in our immature way. The explication phase made me see the tenacity, perseverance, and determination it took to stand together against the adult world, even if what we saw was more perception than fact. Our perceptions were subjective because we only saw each incident out of context and did not fully understand the surrounding context. For instance, what made it was possible for an adult to gain access to us and why the neighbors were only trying to protect their own children, instead of being concerned for our welfare.

Three of the many key characteristics found in leaders are *courage* to proceed and take the consequences; *perseverance* in the face of adversity; and *determination* to make it through a real or imaginary threat or opportunity. Two of the elements identified by the resiliency theorists as protective factors are adaptation and self-efficacy. Adaptation was the strongest protective factor for most of us and was also the one that found our Achilles heel. Adaptation as a protective factor was our ability to adapt in many situations when we were unable to find an adult champion to protect us from our abusers. Adaptation sought out and found our Achilles heel when it came to wounding our egos and inner spirits. Outwardly we each showed the courage to fight back while trying to keep the internal messages at bay. In many cases, these feelings were demonstrated through attempted suicides, bed wetting, sucking thumbs, nail biting and eating disorders. We were older children ages 8 through 14, when we unknowingly learned self-efficacy. Self-efficacy is the protective element that allows an individual to attain certain goals. We all were still able to socially interact with our friends and relations in almost every way. What some of us lacked was a method for how to develop the ability to create more productive, happy lives.

Recognizing how time erodes memory, causing my mind to distort the past, it was necessary to find corroborators. Health issues were a concern. At the time, my eighty-two year old father appeared to be in fair shape, even though he was required to go for dialysis twice a week. During this time my youngest sister lived near me, however she was also going to dialysis. I was also concerned about obtaining verifications. An even larger concern during this research was maintaining my boundaries and preventing my personal biases from entering into the retelling of family members' stories. This limitation is identified by Merriam (1998) who acknowledges that a researcher is human and as a human instrument is limited by their humanity. To summarize Merriam's (1998, p.20) statement, a human instrument is prone to make mistakes, miss opportunities, and allow one's own personal biases to enter the picture. As Merriam writes, "Human instruments are as fallible as any other research instrument."

Recognizing these challenges, I was prepared to find ways to maintain objectivity such as using a videotape camera to interview my father, and reading what I had written out loud to family members for their feedback. To authenticate my memory, I researched and found relevant articles on the internet, as well as correcting or adding my families' perceptions of the same time period. Finally, to help validate the stories, I collected old photographs as well as acquiring case studies on trauma for use as references.

The only way to avoid projecting my own memories was to conduct face-to-face interviews and phone conversations with those family members who lived at long distances from me. It was during the explication phase that I learned why my father left me at the hospital and how my sister was able to survive her two suicide attempts. Their explanations and other responses to my questions, provided me with new information and expanded my memory of certain incidents in my mind.

Creative Synthesis

This final phase was truly experienced throughout the writing of *Saving the Leader Within*, with the poetry or notable quotes at the beginning of each chapter, ending with my own poem that I wrote during the illumination and explication phases. The need to express myself through different mediums has been a constant for me, even as a child. It was my self-expression through visual arts that caught my first mentor's eye. It was through dance that I rechanneled my raw angry emotions through movement. Just as writing this book is a strong expression of my freedom from what formerly kept the curtain of silence in place.

The process of using a self-discovering inquiry can assist leaders who are trauma survivors to uncover facets of their own lives and help them to begin their healing process as it has helped me. According to DeFrain et al., (2003, p. 2)

After studying more than 2,500 pages of written testimony from 90 individuals describing how they believe they have survived and transcended a traumatic childhood, the researchers conclude that human beings are capable of healing from horrendous emotional wounds. However, the journey to health is a long and difficult one, and the early negative experiences appear to be woven into the individual's very soul, perhaps for as long as the person is alive.

DeFrain's above statement is true in my experience; it requires constant vigilance for me to stay conscious of what took place in the past and what in some cases has been distorted by memory and through the passage of time. I am a better person for taking this journey and value my last experiences with my decreased father and sisters now having clearer and healthier memories.

REFERENCES

Angelou, M. (1993). *Wouldn't Take Nothing For My Journey Now*. New York: Random House p. 33-34.

Arunga-Tate, M. (2002). "Exploration into the Process of Cultural Reconnection for African American Women" Thesis presented at Pacific Oaks University: Seattle, WA (Chapter 4, p. 59)

Baker-Pierce, C. (1998). Surviving the Silence: Black Women's Stories of *Rape*. New York, NY: W.W. Norton and Company

Bandura, A., & Adams, N.E. (1977). Analysis of self-efficacy theory and behavioral change. Cognitive Therapy and Research, I, 287-310

Bandura, A. (1986). Social Foundations of Thought and Action: A Social Cognitive View. Englewood Cliffs: NJ Prentice-Hall

Bandura, A. (1991). Social cognitive theory of moral thought and action. In W.M. Kurtines & J. L. Gewirtz (Eds.), *Handbook of moral behavior and development* (Vol. 1, p. 45-103). Hillsdale, NJ: Erlbaum Banks, J. A., & Banks, C. A. M. (2004). *Multicultural Education: Issues and Perspectives* (5th Ed.) Hoboken, NJ: John Wiley & Sons, Inc.

Bass, Bernard, M., (1990) Bass and Stogdill's Handbook of Leadership: Theories, Research and Managerial Approaches., published by The Free Press

Bass, E., & Davis, L. (1988). The Courage to Heal: A Guide for Women Survivors of Child Sexual Abuse. (3rd Ed.). Santa Cruz, CA: Harper Perennial.

Berg, J. C. (1994). Unequal Struggle: Class, Gender, Race, and Power in U.S. Congress. Boulder, CO: Westview Press

Brooks, R., & Goldstein, S. (2004). *The Power of Resilience.* New York, NY: Contemporary Books

Brown, C. S. (2002). Refusing Racism: White Allies and the Struggle for Civil Rights. New York, NY: Teachers College Press

Burgess, G.J. (2006). Legacy Living: The Six Covenants for Personal & *Professional Excellence.* Provo, UT: Executive Excellence Publishing

Burns, J. M. (1978). Leadership. New York, NY: Harper Torchbooks

Cameron, J. (1997). Heart Steps: Prayers and Declarations for a Creative *Life.* New York, NY: Penguin Putnam, Inc.

Carson, C., Shepard, K., Young, A. (Ed.) (2001). A Call to Conscience: Landmark Speeches of Martin Luther King Jr. New York, NY: IPM Warner

Carson, C. (ed.) (1999.) The Autobiography of Martin Luther King Jr. New York, NY: ABACUS

Casey, B., L. (2001). "Resiliency Factors and Performance on the Washington State Essential Learning Exam: Psychosocial Issues and Academic Achievement of Students at Risk." Educational Leadership, School of *Education*. Seattle, WA, Seattle University: 129.

Cato, Doreen (2004, May). Poverty and Education: What messages are we giving our children? Paper presented at 2005 Seattle University Leadership Conference, Seattle, WA

Chomsky, N. (1988). Language and Problems of Knowledge. Cambridge, MA: The MIT Press. Copage, E. V. (1993). Black Pearls: Daily Mediations, Affirmations, and Inspirations for African-Americans. New York, NY: Quill, William Morrow and Company, Inc.

Cook, B. W. (1992). Eleanor Roosevelt: Volume one 1884-1933. New York: Penguin Books

DA Capo (Ed). (1992). *The Autobiography of Eleanor Roosevelt.* New York, NY: The DA Capo Press

Davis, J.E. (2005). Accounts of Innocence: Sexual Abuse, Trauma, and the *Self.* Chicago, IL: The University of Chicago Press

DeFrain, J., Jones, J., Skogrand, L., Ernst, L., DeFrain, N. (2003). Surviving and Transcending a Traumatic Childhood: An Exploratory

Study" NE: University of Nebraska Press, Project #NEB92-026. ARD Journal Series Number 12153: Retrieved from the internet November 12,2006,unlforfamilies.unl.edu/Publications/Surviving And Transcending Traumatic Childhood

Eubanks, S. (2002). Quotable King: Words of Wisdom, Inspiration, and Freedom by and About Dr. Martin Luther King Jr. Nashville, TN: Towelhouse Publishing Company.

Erikson, E.H. (1963). Childhood and Society. (2nd Ed.). New York: Norton . . . . Erikson, E. H. (1968). Identity: Youth and crisis. New York: Norton

Erikson, E. H. (1999). Identity's Architect: A Biography of Erik H. Erikson. New York, NY: Simon and Shuster

Everson, T. (1994). Resiliency and skill-building: A spiritual perspective. Journal of Emotional and Behavioral Problems, vol. 3, 25-29.

Flavell, J. H. (1976). Meta-Cognitive Dimensions of Problem-solving, The Nature of Intelligence. Hillsdale, NJ: Hyson, Marion C. (1994), *The Emotional Development of Young Children: Building and Emotion-Centered Curriculum* (New York: Teachers College Press).

Frady, M. (2002). *Martin Luther King, Jr., A Life.* New York, NY: The Penguin Group Freire, P. (3rd Ed.). (2003). *Pedagogy of the Oppressed.* New York, NY: The Continuum International Publishing Group, Inc.

Gall, J.P., Gall, M.D., & Borg, W. R. (4th Ed.). (1999). *Applying Educational Research: A Practical Guide.* New York, NY: Addison Wesley Longman, Inc.

Gardner, H. (1995). *Leading Minds: An Anatomy of Leadership.* New York, NY: BasicBooks

Gardner, H. (1991). The Unschooled Mind: How Children Think & How *Schools Should Teach.* New York, NY: BasicBooks.

Gardner, John W. (1990). *On Leadership.* New York, NY: The Free Press

Garner, R. (1994). Meta-cognition and Executive control, *Theoretical Models And Processes of Reading,* (4th Ed.) Newark, DE: International Reading Association

Gates, H. L., Jr. (2004). *America Behind the Color Line.* New York, N.Y.: Warner Books

Gendler, R. J. (1988). *The Book of Qualities.* NY: Harper Perennial.

Gendler, R. J. (1991). Changing Light: The Eternal Cycle of Night and Day. New York, NY: HarperCollins Publisher.

Giroux, H.A. (1997). Pedagogy and the Politics of Hope: Theory, Culture, *and Schooling.* Boulder, CO: Westview Press

Goldstein, S., & Brooks, R. B. (2005). *Handbook of Resilience in Children.* New York, NY: Kluwer Academic/Plenum Publishers

Greene, R.R., (Ed.). (2002). Resiliency: An Integrated Approach to Practice, *Policy, and Research.* Washington D.C.: National Association of Social Workers (NASW) Press

Hall, B. P. (1994). Values Shift: A Guide to Personal & Organizational *Transformation._*Rockport, MA: Twin Lights Publishers

Harrington, R., Fudge, H., Rutter, M., Pickles, A., & Hill, J. (1990). Adult outcomes of childhood and adolescent depression: Psychiatric status. Archives of General Psychiatry, 47, 465-473

Harris, M. (1998). Trauma Recovery and Empowerment: A Clinician's Guide for Working with Women in Groups. New York, NY: The Free Press

Hayakawa, S. I., & Hayakawa, A.R. (1990). Language in Thought and Action. Orlando, FL: Harcourt, Inc.

Heifetz, R. A. (1994). *Leadership Without Easy Answers.* Cambridge, MA: The Belknap Press of Harvard University Press

Herman, J., M.D. (1997). Trauma and Recovery: The aftermath of violence from domestic abuse to political terror. New York, NY: Basic Books hooks, b. (1996). *Bone Black: Memories of Girlhood.* New York, NY: Henry Holt and Company

James, B. (1989). Treating Traumatized Children: New Insights and Creative *Interventions*. New York, NY: The Free Press

Jaworski, J. (1996). Synchronicity: The Inner Path of Leadership. San Francisco, CA: Berrett-Koehler Publisher.

Jones, M. L. (1993). *The Color of Culture*. Seattle, WA: Impact Communications

Kersey, David and Bates, Marilyn (1978). *Please Understand Me: Character and Temperament Types*. New York, NY, Prometheus Nemesis Book Company

King, M. L., Jr. Dr. (1967). Where Do We Go from Here: Chaos or *Community?* New York, NY, Beacon Press Books.

Knutson, J.E. (1974). The Human Basis of the Polity: A Psychological Study of Political Men. *The American Political Science Review*, Vol. 68, No. 1. Chicago, IL: Aldine Press

Kyle, E. C. (1988). *Unbeatable Bessie: A Biography of Bessie Kidd Best*. Huntington, WV: Aegina Press,

Leary, J. D. Ph.D. (2005). *Post Traumatic Slave Syndrome*. Milwaukie, OR: Upton Press.

Lifton, R. J. (1993). The protean self: Human resilience in an age of *fragmentation*. Chicago, IL: University of Chicago Press

Macedo, D. & Bartolome, L. I., (1999). *Dancing with Bigotry: Beyond the Politics of Tolerance.* New York, NY: Palgrave

Maggio, R. (1996). The New Beacon Book of Quotations By Women. Boston, MA: The Beacon Press

Maloba, Wunyabari O. (1993). MAU MAU and Kenya: An Analysis of a Peasant Revolt. Bloomington, IN: Indiana University Press

Martin, E. P & Martin, J. M. (1978). The Black Extended Family. Chicago, IL: The University of Chicago Press Marshall, F. (2002). Martin Luther King Jr.: A Life. New York, NY: Penguin Group McKenna, B. (2005). Our Hearts Our Stories: Twenty-Nine Stories Filled with Laughter, Love, and Triumph. Seattle, WA: Dress for Success

Maathai, W. (2006). *Unbowed: A Memoir.* New York, NY: Random House Publishers

McKnight, R. (ed.) 1994). *African-American Wisdom.* San Rafael, CA: New World Library Merriam, S. & Simpson, E. (2000). A Guide to Research for Educators and *Trainers of Adults.* Malabar, Fl, Krieger Publishing Company.

Merriam, S. B. (1998). Qualitative Research and Case Study Applications in *Education.* San Francisco, CA: Jossey-Bass Publishers Miles, M. B., Huberman, M. A. (1994). *Qualitative Data Analysis.* Thousand Oaks, CA: Sage Publications

Moustakas, C. (1990). Heuristic Research: Design, Methodology, and *Applications.* Newberry Park, CA, Sage Publications, Inc. Painter, N. I. (1996). *Sojourner Truth: A Life, A Symbol.* New York, N.Y.: W.W. Norton and Company

Palmer, P.J. (2000). Let Your Life Speak: Listening for the Voice of Vocation. San Francisco, CA: Jossey-Bass Palmer, P.J. (2004). A Hidden Wholeness: The Journey Toward An Undivided *Life.* San Francisco, CA: Jossey-Bass

Palmer, P.J. (2005). *Living the Questions.* San Francisco, CA: Jossey-Bass

Patterson, S. & Wu, S. M. (Ed.). (2000). Lift Every Voice: Words of Black Wisdom and Celebration New York, NY: Barnes and Nobles Books Pearlman, L. A., & Saakvitne, K. W. (1995a). Trauma and the therapist: Counter transference and vicarious traumatization in psychotherapy with incest survivors. New York: Norton.

Perrucci, R., Wysong, E. (1999). *The New Class Society.* Lanham, MA: Rowman and Littlefield Publishers, Inc.Pena, R. A., Guest, K. A., Matsuda, L. (2005). *Community and Difference: Teaching Pluralism, And Social Justice.* Portland, OR: Peter Lang Publisher, Inc. Pfeiffer, William J., (1991). Theories and Models in Applied Behavioral *Science,* Volume I. Pfeiffer and Company, p. 241

Richardson, R. W. (1995). Family Ties that Bind: A Self-help guide to change through Family of Origin therapy. Bellingham, WA: Self-Counsel Press

Rubin, G. (2003). *Forty Ways to Look at Winston Churchill: A Brief Account of a Long Life.* New York, NY: The Random House Ballantine Publishing Group

Russell, K., Wilson, M., & Hall, R. (1992). *The Color Complex: the Politics of Skin Color among African Americans.* Orlando, FL: Harcourt Brace Jovanovich Publishers

Shaka, O. T. (1990). *The Art of Leadership.* Richmond, CA: Pan Afrikan Publications

Sauter, V. G. B., H. (1968). Nightmare in Detroit; A Rebellion and its Victims. Chicago, IL, Regency Publishers.

Tatum, B.D., Ph.D. (1999). Why All the Black Kids Sitting Together in the *Cafeteria?* New York, NY: Basic Books

Thurman, H. (1989). *The Luminous Darkness.* New York, NY: Harper & Row

Ungar, M. (2004). Nurturing Hidden Resilience in Troubled Youth. Toronto, Canada: University of Toronto Press

Vanzant, I. (1995). *Interiors: A Black Woman's Healing in Progress.* New \ York, NY: Writers and Readers Publishing, Inc.

Viscott, D., M.D. (1996). Emotional Resilience: Simple Truths for Dealing with the Unfinished Business of your Past. New York, NY:

Three Rivers Press Wink, J. (1997). Critical Pedagogy: Notes from the Real World. White Plains, NY: Longman Publishers USA

Yukl, Gary (2002). *Leadership In Organizations*, Fifth Edition, Pearson Education, Inc., Chapter 10, p. 279

Text citations

Brooks & Goldstein (2003) on the study of resilience in children

Benson, P.L., Galbraith, J. & Espeland, P. (1995). What Kids Need to Succeed. Minneapolis, MN: Free Spirit

Conrad, A. R. Ph.D. & Greene, R. R. (1999). Resiliency: An integrated approach to practice, policy, and Research. Washington, DC: NASW Press, pp. 29-62.

Egeland, B., Carlson, E., & Sroufe, L.A. (1993). Resilience as process. *Development and Psychopathology*, 5, 517-528.

Maloba, W. (1998). Mau Mau and Kenya: An Analysis of a peasant revolt. Indiana: Indiana University Press

Masten, A.S., Best, K.M., & Garmezy, N. (1990). Resilience and development: Contributions from the study of children who overcome adversity. *Development and Psychopathology*, 2, 425-444.

Masten, A.S., & Wright, M. O'D. (1997 in press). Cumulative risk and protection models of child maltreatment. In B.B.R.

Rossman, & M.S. Rosenberg (Eds.), *multiple victimization of children: Conceptual, developmental, research and treatment issues.* Binghampton, NY: Haworth Press.

Garmezy, N., & Masten, A.S. (1994). Chronic adversities. In M. Rutter, L. Herzov, & E. Taylor (Eds.), *Child and Adolescent Psychiatry* (3rd ed.; pp. 191-208) Oxford: Blackwell.

Citations by Brown, C. S. (2002). Refusing Racism: White Allies and the Struggle for Civil Rights. New York, NY: Teachers College Press

Blaut, J. M. (1993). The colonizer's model of the world: Geographical diffusionism and Eurocentric history. New York: Guilford Press

Mills, C. W. (1997). *The racial contract.* Ithaca, NY: Cornell University Press Citations by Roberta R. Greene (2002). Resiliency: An integrated Approach to Practice, Policy, and Research

Benard, B. (1997). *Turning it around for all youth: From risk to resilience* (ERIC Clearinghouse on Urban Education, Institute for Urban and Minority Education, No. 126). Available: http://eric-web. tc.columbia.edu/digests/dig126.html.

McAdoo, H. P. (1992). Upward mobility and parenting in middle-income black families. IN H. Burlew, W.C. Banks, H. P. McAdoo, & D. A. Azibo (Eds.), *African American psychology: Theory, research, and practice* (p. 63-86). Newbury Park, CA: Sage Publications.

Miller, D. B., & MacIntosh, R. (1999). Promoting resilience in urban African American adolescents:; Racial socialization and identity as protective factors. *Social Work Research*, 23, 159-170.

Rutter, M. (1985). Resilience in the face of adversity: Protective factors and resistance to psychiatric disorder. *British Journal of Psychiatry*, 147, 598-611.

Williams, N.R. (2002). Surviving Violence: Resiliency in Action at the Micro Level. Washington, DC: National Association of Social Workers (NASW) Press (p. 195-215)

Website

Hersey, J. (1967). 12ᵗʰ Street Riot, Time Magazine. New York, NY: Warner Communications, Inc. Retrieved from the internet in December 28, 2004 www.geocities.com/mich**detroit/riot1967.** html

Livingston, J. A. (1996). *Effects of metacognitive instruction on strategy use of college students.* Unpublished manuscript, State University of New York at Buffalo. Retrieved on December 26, 2006 from www. gse.buffalo.edu/fas/shuell/CEP564/Metacog.htm

Masten, A. (1997). Resilience in Children At-Risk. Institute of Child Development, College of Education and Human Development, University of Minnesota. Retrieved January 15, 2007, from the University of Minnesota, Research and Practice Newsletter.

www.education.umn.edu/CAREI/Reports/Rpractice/Spring97/resilience.html.

Miller, A. (1998). Retrieved from the internet March 18, 2007 www.vachss.com/guest_dispatches/alice_miller2.html

Phenomenology: Stanford Encyclopedia of Philosophy retrieved on June 27, 2006 from http://plato.stanford.edu/entries/phenomenology

Unbeatable Bessie Best: Biography of Bessie Best, retrieved from the web on March 30, 2007 from www.ic.arizona.edu/ic/mcbride/ws200/mine-hist.htm

Theses and Papers

Livingston, J. (1997) Metacognition: An Overview taken from Effects of Metacognitive Instruction on Strategy Use of College Students written in 1996: Unpublished manuscript, State University of New York at Buffalo. *http://gse.buffalo.edu/fas/shuell/CEP564/metacog.htm*

Shonkoff, J.P. & Phillips, D.A. (Ed.) (2000). From Neurons to Neighborhoods: The Science of Early Childhood Development. Board on Children, Youth, and Families National Research Council and Institute of Medicine, Washington, D.C.: National Academy Press.